17 Things Resilient Teachers Do

This book will help you learn practical ways to manage the stress of teaching and avoid burnout. Bestselling author and educational consultant Bryan Harris presents strategies for building resilience, including reframing, understanding the power of "no", focusing on what you can control, building positive relationships, advocating for yourself, and more. Each chapter clearly presents concise and practical applications that you can implement right away. With this guidebook, you'll feel ready to bounce back from challenges and stay focused on the joys of the profession.

Bryan Harris is an education consultant, author, and former Director of Professional Development and Public Relations for the Casa Grande Elementary School District in Arizona. He previously held positions as a teacher, district-level specialist, and principal.

T0386418

17 Things Resilient Teachers Do

(And 4 Things They Hardly Ever Do)

Bryan Harris

Routledge
Taylor & Francis Group

NEW YORK AND LONDON

First published 2021
by Routledge
52 Vanderbilt Avenue, New York, NY 10017

and by Routledge
2 Park Square, Milton Park, Abingdon, Oxon, OX14 4RN

Routledge is an imprint of the Taylor & Francis Group, an informa business

Library of Congress Cataloging-in-Publication Data
A catalog record for this title has been requested

ISBN: 978-0-367-52844-7 (hbk)
ISBN: 978-0-367-52036-6 (pbk)
ISBN: 978-1-003-05864-9 (ebk)

Typeset in Palatino
by codeMantra

To educators everywhere. Thanks for what you do.

Contents

Acknowledgments

No book is complete without recognizing the efforts of those individuals who provided support, guidance, and friendship.

- ♦ To my wife Becky and my sons Andrew and Jeremy, you've allowed me to be myself (dad jokes and all), which has helped me discover more about what it means to be resilient. To my mom and my sister, as a child, I began learning what it meant to be resilient because of your examples. I'm blessed to have a family that loves me and accepts for me who I am.
- ♦ To my professional support network of Shauna King and LeAnn Nickelsen, you've been a constant source of encouragement and support. You two are more than professional colleagues who steal good ideas from me; you are also friends.
- ♦ To my friends Scott Taylor and Kurt Morris, you do more than tolerate my bad jokes; you encourage and you care. Scott is a constant example of a person who chooses to see the good in life, and Kurt is a living example of what it means to practice resilience in the midst of life's challenges.
- ♦ To my church family, as imperfect as we are, you are a constant source of encouragement and light.
- ♦ To the giants in the field of stress and resiliency research, this book stands on your shoulders.
- ♦ To the wonderfully supportive team at Routledge, led by my long-time editor Lauren Davis, thanks for believing in yet another project.

About the Author

I always hate writing bios. It's hard not to sound like I'm bragging, and I often wonder if people even read them.

If you're interested, here's what you might want to know.

I'm a life-long educator who loves his family, loves God, and is doing his best to better the lives of educators and students.

Along the way, I've served in a variety of roles, including classroom teacher, school principal, district-level director, and adjunct professor. In the process, I accumulated a few college degrees.

I now work as a full-time educational consultant, focusing on teacher effectiveness and student engagement. I first got interested in the topic of stress and resiliency when I was conducting doctoral research focused on new-teacher retention. For that, and personal reasons, I wanted to learn how to become more resilient myself.

This isn't my first book and hopefully won't be my last.

On a personal note, I'm just a normal, super-nice guy who has been tremendously blessed as a result of hard work, the grace and patience of other people, a deep desire to learn and improve, and a bit of serendipity.

One *more* note – I'm not sure if this is your thing or not, but if you like the ideas presented in this book, a positive online review would be appreciated. You likely already know this, but success in the book business is largely measured by Amazon reviews and sales rankings. My goal is to share these ideas with as many people as possible. Positive reviews help to achieve that goal.

You can find out more by visiting my website – www.bryan-harris.com – and by following me on Twitter – @bryankharris7. While I'm at it, you might also want to know how to be in touch, in case you are looking for training or support for your staff, school district, or organization. Email is always a great way to reach out – bryan@bryan-harris.com.

Introduction

Here's the big idea – If you are to become the superstar teacher you were meant to be, you have to take care of yourself. You have to develop, refine, and practice resilience. This book will show you how.

Teaching is hard. It's awesome, but hard. As educators, our days are filled with highs and lows, triumphs and challenges, joys and sorrows. Quite simply, teaching is an emotionally taxing, tremendously rewarding roller coaster of a job.

For those of us who have dedicated our lives to the education of young people, we know this essential truth – while teaching is the most rewarding job on the planet, it's also one of the most exhausting. It's not like other jobs. Make no mistake, there are lots of other professions that are both rewarding and challenging, but teaching is unique. Shaping the lives of children is unlike any other job in existence.

Because of the uniquely demanding and emotionally taxing nature of the profession, we need to develop, refine, and practice the art of resiliency. In order to be the very best teachers we can be, we must be resilient. Here's the main message: taking care of yourself is not selfish. In fact, it's essential. Whether you refer to it as self-care, emotional resourcefulness, equanimity, fortitude, or grit, the idea is the same. In order to take care of others – in order to be that world-class educator you aspire to be – you must take care of yourself by building your own capacity to handle stress. We deal with stress by practicing resiliency.

So, what is resilience? Words and concepts commonly associated with resilience include: persistence, the ability to "bounce back" after a setback, the ability to cope during times of adversity, and the capacity to navigate difficult waters. At its most basic, resilience is made up of those mindsets/beliefs/internal values we possess along with a set of specific strategies we employ during the tough times. Resiliency is two things: how we think and what we do. For those of us who work in schools, resiliency can be viewed as using our skills, energy, and abilities to do the best for ourselves and our students in the face of (*sometimes*) adverse conditions.

Is there evidence that you can grow and improve your personal resilience? Well, yes there is. Quite a bit of it actually, and we'll tackle some of it throughout this book. Simply put, while we are all born with varying degrees of resilience, and through intentional practice, we can improve (Schiraldi et al., 2010). And, teachers who are resilient experience less stress and burnout (Richards et al., 2016).

In what is probably the best book available on the topic of building teacher resiliency (besides this one, of course), educator Elena Aguilar reminds us that resiliency isn't just about surviving the tough times. In *Onward - Cultivating Emotional Resilience in Educators* (2018), Aguilar points out that resilience is an adaptive process that equips us not just to survive, but to thrive. The goal is not simply to have a set of tools that allow us to weather the storm; the goal is to also equip us with a set of tools that helps us to thrive, despite stressful circumstances.

Being resilient is about how we react to life's challenges. As my mother often says, "Life is how you handle plan B". It's not a matter of *if* there will be challenges in your life, or your career, or your relationships, or your health, or… (the list could go on, but you get the point). It's a matter of *when* those challenges will present themselves. The central question is this, "*How prepared are you to tackle those challenges?*" Resilient people know their strengths and they know what coping mechanisms and tools to use during those challenging times.

This book is part resource, part motivational kick in the pants, and part exercise in reflection on one's life and career. It will equip you with specific tools (17 of them, in fact) and will take you on a journey to consider what tools and skills you already possess as well as help you to discover where you might improve. Resilience comes from the repeated practice of effective habits and strategies (Hanson, 2018). You learn resiliency the same way you learn anything: focus, attention, trial and error, feedback, and reflection.

Most of the strategies and techniques I'll share are surprisingly ordinary and simple. Note that I didn't describe the strategies as *easy*; simple and easy are not the same thing. They are simple in the sense that they are straightforward and easy to comprehend. Putting the strategies and techniques into practice in your daily life is the challenge. But you already know the price of not managing your stress: burnout, frustration, hopelessness, and exhaustion.

This book will equip you with the tools to manage stress and love your job. There is a chapter devoted to each of the 17 things. In each chapter, I'll give you the big-picture idea (*In a Nutshell*); I'll share insights, evidence, research, and anecdotes (*Digging Deeper*); and, perhaps most importantly, I'll share specific strategies and techniques to build and practice resilience (*Application Points*). Here is my promise – we'll keep it real, we'll keep it relevant, we'll make it practical, and we'll keep it light-hearted. Building and practicing resiliency is serious business, but we can have a little bit of fun along the way as well.

One last note before we jump into the good stuff. I researched and wrote this book partially because I needed it. Not because I had any major life blow or overwhelming tragedy to deal with, but because the more I learned about stress and resiliency, the more I wanted a concise, accurate, and easy-to-understand tool to help me wrap my head around these important concepts. And, I needed to practice these concepts in my own life before I preached them to others. With that said, dive in and give them a shot. You'll be glad you did.

OK, one *more* note before we dig in – the 17 ideas outlined here are guidelines, not rules. Don't consider these ideas as a checklist of things you have to do. Rather, consider them as powerful ideas that, when regularly practiced, improve your ability to thrive through the challenges. The more you make these ideas a regular part of your thinking and coping, the more fulfillment and fun you'll have in your job.

Stress Is the Issue
Here Is What You Need to Know

To tackle the concept of stress in one short chapter is a challenge, but we'll give it a shot. Countless books, articles, research studies, and expert opinions have weighed in on the topic. While we are still learning (and there is still much *to* learn), there is agreement on a few things that are important for our understanding of how to manage stress and build personal resilience.

To start, let's figure out what we are talking about – *What is stress? Why does it matter? What is the relationship to resiliency?*

For our purposes here, we'll adopt Dr. Eric Jensen's (2005) definition of stress – *the physiological response to a perception of a lack of control over an adverse situation or person.* There are two key terms in this definition that you'll see as reoccurring themes throughout this book: perception and control.

First, stress is perception. And, that perception is highly variable; people can respond very differently to similar situations based on what they believe and perceive (Levitin, 2020). In other words, there is no stress outside of your own perception of it. Think about it this way – is skydiving stressful? Think about strapping on a parachute, getting into a plane, going up to 13,000 feet, and jumping. Is that a stressful event? Some of you are saying, *"Heck yeah it's stressful. There's no way I'd do that"*, while others might say, *"Sounds fun. Let's go"*. The key idea is that skydiving is just a thing. Stress is really about what we perceive or believe about a situation and no two people respond the same way (Medina, 2008).

The second reoccurring theme you'll see throughout this book centers on control. In fact, the concept of control might just be *the* theme. Most of the experts and organizations who study stress (Bruce McEwan, Robert Sapolsky, The American Institute of Stress, and may others) key in on this very important idea: stress is related to control. Very specifically, it is related to the perception of control. This is one of the central messages of the entire book: in order to manage the stressors that are inherent with the job, get control. The strategies and coping mechanisms I'll describe center on this idea: to manage stress, take action and focus on what you can control.

Why does all this matter? It's quite simple, really. Unchecked stress is killing you. It's wreaking havoc on your physical health, your mental stability, your relationships, and even on your finances and future security. And, oh yeah – unchecked stress makes you miserable at work. It leads to burnout, exhaustion, and has you wondering if the local Piggly Wiggly has any openings for cashiers. We'll talk more in Chapter 1 about how unchecked stress impacts your physical health, but here is a spoiler alert: it's not good.

It should be clarified, however, that not all stress is bad. In fact, some stress is good for you. Daniel Amen, in *Making a Good Brain Great* (2005) reminds us that stress can be either good or bad. Good stress can motivate us to pay attention to something important. In essence, he says, *if it stresses you out, you ought to be paying attention to it*. That's the role of stress after all – to focus your attention on something related to your safety or survival. Temporary and manageable stress (we can call that good stress) can motivate us to take action, while long-term unchecked stress can literally kill us. If you think I'm being a bit dramatic here, maybe I am. But keep reading, this stuff is relevant and might very well change your life.

When you feel stress – when you perceive that something is beyond your control – the brain and body respond in a very specific way by releasing a host of chemicals (primarily cortisol and adrenaline) that are designed with one very specific purpose: to equip you with the physical and mental resources necessary to gain a sense of control. The process is started in the brain's limbic system, which is designed to detect threat and promote survival.

Many researchers describe stress in this manner: it is the body's response to a situation where the demands exceed the current resources. The American Institute of Stress defines it this way – stress is a "condition or feeling experienced when a person perceives that demands exceed the personal and social resources the individual is able to mobilize".

Although a bit simplistic, it goes something like this: you find yourself in a situation, relationship, or context where you perceive that you'll have little or no control. The external demands of the situation are greater than the current resources you have to deal with it. So, your brain and body respond by saying, "*OK, we've got a problem. We don't have the kind of control we want. So, let's open the reserves of adrenaline and cortisol so that we can get some control*". You perceive you don't have the kind of control you want (that is, you feel stressed) so the brain responds by saying, "*Here you go. Here are the resources you need to get some control*".

As your brain "throttles up" and prepares to deal with the stressor (by releasing the likes of cortisol and adrenaline), some cool things happen: your focus and attention is increased, you gain physical energy, your memory improves, and you basically go into problem-solving mode (Sapolsky, 2004). In the short term, this response is great.

The problems occur, as you probably already guessed, when we experience long-term, unchecked stress. Short-term stress is just fine. It's when stress becomes prolonged that we see problems. We use terms like *acute stress, chronic stress*, or *distress* to describe the unhealthy aspects of stress. Basically, stress becomes a problem when it sticks around for too long. When your body and brain are marinating in cortisol for long periods of time, that's when problems occur.

In *Why Zebras Don't Get Ulcers* (the seminal book on the topic of stress), Robert Sapolsky (2004) highlights that stress is not just a brain and body reaction to a challenge or a perception of a lack of control, stress is also the *anticipation* of a challenge. In other words, the stress response kicks in when we have an experience *and* when we anticipate that something will be out of whack.

A stressor, says Sapolsky, is anything that knocks us out of homeostasis (the stable, healthy state our body wants to maintain). In other words, a stressor is something that overwhelms the system. When your brain senses that something is beyond your ability to cope, it floods the body with hormones that are designed to tackle the pending challenge. The whole process is designed to get you back to that stable, healthy state that scientists call homeostasis. But for many of us, we never get back to that healthy state because of the constant stressors we are under. As a result, we experience *allostasis*. That's a term coined by Dr. Bruce McEwan in the 1990s to describe the phenomenon of the brain's adaptability to stress. While our brain and body want to get back to a healthy state after dealing with a stressor, it sometimes doesn't happen. The long-term effect of cortisol changes our brain and causes a "new baseline" called allostasis.

If you've read this far, you might be saying, *"Bryan, I wasn't all that stressed out until I read this. Now I'm really stressed out"*. OK, now that I've stressed you out about stress, let's talk business.

- ◆ Remember that some stress is actually good for you. In short, manageable doses, stress helps you to solve problems and tackle the challenges in front of you. Cortisol (the stress hormone) and adrenaline help with focus, energy, and memory. The problem is when we have un-mediated stress that hangs around for a while. In the short term, cortisol is great. When it stays in your system for a long period of time, it does serious damage.
- ◆ The truth is that teaching *is a special kind of stressful*. What we do matters tremendously for students, for families, and for society in general. A lot rides on how effective we are at our jobs. Part of that effectiveness depends on how well we manage stress.
- ◆ As you read the ideas and suggestions throughout the book, keep in mind our two central ideas: perception and control. If you had control over a situation (or you perceived that you did), it wouldn't be stressful in the first place.
- ◆ If stress is the problem, resiliency is the answer. When we build, practice, and refine our resiliency skills, we become better equipped to deal with the challenges that come along with classroom life. Resiliency consists of two things: how we think and what we do. It consists of our

mental models, our mindsets, and our beliefs along with a specific set of coping mechanisms.

◆ The goal is not to have zero stress. The goal is to understand the role stress plays and how to best manage it. When you are balanced and resilient, teaching is the best job in the world. When you are not, it can be miserable.

◆ If you don't address the issue of stress management, one of two things is likely to happen. You'll either leave the profession entirely or (perhaps worse), you'll stay and be burned out. Resiliency helps us to stay sane and satisfied in a sometimes-insane profession.

◆ Realize that the suggestions highlighted in each of the 17 things are just that – suggestions. They are not mandates. In fact, if you view these ideas as mandates, as a checklist of things you have to do, you've lost control. You've lost sight of the very thing that helps you to manage stress. You control what you do, how you think, and the specific steps you'll take.

1

Resilient Teachers Take Care of Their Health

In a Nutshell: Taking care of yourself – attending to your physical health – is job #1. When you're healthy, the very best of you can be on display. When you are not healthy, it's tough to be your best.

Digging Deeper: As I shared in the chapter on stress, if we don't take care of ourselves, one of two things is likely to happen – we'll either quit and look for a less stressful job or we'll stay in the profession and be burned out. Neither is a good choice. Truly, the best place to begin to manage stress and build resiliency is by taking care of your physical health.

There is a lot of talk, rightfully so, about how we can help prevent teacher burnout. Certainly, there are systemic and structural issues (such as workload and long hours) that lead to high levels of burnout among teachers, but the fact is that *each of us can help prevent our own burnout*. By taking care of yourself – by giving attention to your physical health, you can prevent some of those stressors from getting the best of you. As Elena Aguilar says, "renew yourself" and don't always rely on others to develop conditions that make your life better. Take charge and take control – manage those stressors and prevent burnout by taking care of your physical health.

The evidence is overwhelming. One of the world's leading experts on the impact of stress on health, Dr. Robert Sapolsky, offers a stark (if not slightly humorous) summary of what high levels of stress does to your physical health. Among other things, high stress: raises your blood pressure, damages white blood cells, does damage to your brain, lowers libido, and even makes you flatulent (Sapolsky, 2004). And, if you didn't already know this, stress is contagious (Oberle and Schonert-Reichl, 2016). That's right, your stress impacts those around you, including your students.

Throughout the book, we'll make lots of references to the brain and mental health. Why is that? Many researchers who study resilience look at aspects of a person's mental health in order to gauge their ability to be resilient in the face of life's challenges. Whether you prefer references to mental health, cognitive health, or overall physical health, the ideas are the same – everything is interconnected. When your brain works well, so does the rest of your life. Dr. Daniel Amen, who has authored over 20 books on brain health, says it succinctly, "When your brain works right, you work right; and when your brain is troubled you are much more likely to have trouble in your life" (Amen, 2005).

For our purposes in this chapter, we'll focus primarily on the role that physical health plays in building resiliency and managing stress. Certainly, your relational, emotional, and spiritual health are also important, but we start with an understanding of how an individual's physical health supports every aspect of life. Specifically, we'll look at three areas: exercise, sleep, and diet.

How Does Exercise Support Resilience?

The first thing we need to realize is that everything is connected, or rather inter-connected. To the brain, there is no separate thing called the body. And vice versa. It is one system that works together - those things that impact our bodies also have an impact on the brain. One of the more exciting findings in recent years concerns the connection between heart and brain health. It turns out that what is good for the heart is also good for the brain (Gardener et al., 2016).

While most of us know the importance of exercise for things like weight management or heart health, it is also important to understand how exercise supports mental health and cognition. For example, adults who regularly exercise have greater mental flexibility (Burzynska et al., 2015). Mental flexibility is needed to thrive as a classroom teacher. It allows us to shift between competing demands, determine which things get our attention, and make decisions regarding the best course of action while under pressure.

Our purpose here isn't to provide an extensive review of the literature highlighting exercise and mental health, but it is good to know that lots of research has shown a correlation between physical and mental health.

Why Is Sleep Important?

From a biological perspective sleep must be important when you consider the fact that you spend 1/3rd of every day doing it. Described as your brain's "rinse cycle", sleep does some amazing things for your overall health.

According to the National Institute of Health, adequate sleep: improves focus and attention, helps to maintain a healthy weight, improves the effectiveness of drugs and medications, and improves mood (2013). There is even evidence that those who get more sleep earn more money (Gibson and Shrader, 2014).

For our purposes here, one very important fact is essential to understand: stress and sleep are related. Elevated cortisol levels disrupt the quality and quantity of sleep (Hirotsu et al., 2015). This makes it a vicious cycle for those who are not dealing very well with stress - we are stressed so we can't sleep and when we can't sleep we are more stressed! Additionally, when we are lacking quality sleep, we become more sensitive to stressors that we might normally be able to deal with effectively (Worley, 2018). Exhaustion isn't evidence of effectiveness. I'll say that again because it is so important - just because we work hard and are tired at the end of the day doesn't mean that we were effective at accomplishing important and essential things.

What Role Does Diet Play in My Ability to Manage Stress?

Our diet impacts every aspect of our lives, not just our waistlines. Remember that the brain and body are interconnected. What is good for the body is good for the brain and vice versa. Without going into a lengthy listing of the relationship between diet and stress, consider just a few key findings from the research: What we eat impacts our mood and mental health (Stranges, 2014); Anxiety disorders are far greater for those with serious weight problems (Davison et al., 2020) and; Intermittent fasting and calorie restriction can increase neuroplasticity and improve cognitive function (van Pragg et al., 2014).

To make a big challenge even bigger, when we are under stress, we often make poor dietary decisions (Oliver et al., 2000). The primary message is this: when it comes to managing stress, consider the impact of your diet. While it may not necessarily be easy, knowing that stress and control are related, what we elect to put into our bodies is certainly under our control.

These topics – exercise, diet, and sleep – aren't so much about trying to gain an ideal weight or a perfect body (although I am still trying to lose those last ten pounds), it is about doing my best to keep my body strong and healthy because a healthy body produces a healthy mind. I need to be as healthy as possible in order to manage the stressors that are inherent in the job. In the book *Thrive* (2020), friend and colleague Dr. Jenny Severson puts it more directly. Regarding your health, she implores us not to wait for a crisis before we take action, "Don't make your health someone else's problem".

Application Points

◆ *Avoid excuses* – Don't justify poor habits by claiming that you don't have the time or money to be healthy. You need to take care of yourself so that you can be healthy enough to take care of other people. My friend, colleague, and fellow educator Shaun King reminds us that, "You can't pour from an empty cup". Fight the urge to find excuses.

Resilient people acknowledge the challenges they face while at the same time working to find ways to meet their personal needs.

♦ *Adopt a "me, too" mindset* – Get on board with the premise that taking care of yourself is not selfish. Rather, it is necessary. Don't feel guilty about taking time to maintain or improve your health. A popular quote from L.R. Knost is a good reminder for all of us, "Taking care of yourself doesn't mean me first, it means me too".

♦ *Move and exercise* – the US Department of Health and Human Services suggests that adults get at least 150 minutes of exercise per week. This could be in the form of walking, weight training, or even yoga. And, no – running after naughty students does not count as exercise.

♦ *Go to sleep* – According to the National Institutes of Health, healthy adults need seven to eight hours of sleep per night.

♦ *Get some rest* – In the book *Burnout: The Secret to Unlocking the Stress Cycle* (2019), sisters Emily and Amelia Nagasaki make a compelling argument that rest is essential to managing stress. Including sleep, they suggest that 42% of each day be made up of rest. They define rest or stress-relieving activities as things like exercise, being with friends and family, reading, eating a healthy meal, and avoiding excessive screen time. "Rest" consists of those things that energize you. The concept of the Sabbath – a day of rest – has legitimacy in this context. If you work 7 days a week, you'll burn out.

♦ *Incorporate a balanced diet* – There are lots of experts and opinions about the best diet plans, so be careful not to jump on the latest trend. Consult your physician about your unique situation and make a plan to incorporate a healthy, balanced diet.

♦ *As a bonus idea* – Teach kids and parents about the importance of sleep. Have kids keep a sleep journal with goal chart like the ones they use with United Way fund drives – a big thermometer. Most parents know, in a general sense, that sleep is important, but if they know just how essential it is, it may provide them with the evidence they need to tackle tough conversations with their kids.

◆ *Another bonus idea* – For those of you who are in leadership positions, it is important to emphasize that we do have an obligation to consider those systems, procedures, or expectations that are placing unnecessary stress on the lives of our teachers. Just because some of them need to do a better job taking care of themselves doesn't get us off the hook for doing our part. Additionally, our school improvement initiatives or curricular changes are not likely to have the impact we expect if teachers are not taking care of themselves. As leaders, we can be a tremendous blessing to our teachers when we help them to take care of themselves. And, we need to be modeling healthy behaviors ourselves (but maybe that's a topic for the next book).

2

Resilient Teachers Practice Gratitude

In a Nutshell: Expressing gratitude builds resiliency by helping to buffer the negative effects of the stressors around us. Quite simply, being grateful improves every aspect of life.

Digging Deeper: Researchers in the social sciences have been studying the power and effects of gratitude for nearly 100 years. Certainly, religious leaders, philosophers, and artists have pondered the concept of gratitude for millennia, but within the last several decades, some serious research has focused on discovering the mechanisms and effects of gratitude. What has been discovered will amaze you; of all human emotions, it turns out that contemplating and expressing gratitude has powerful and lasting effects on overall health and resiliency.

Let's begin by trying to define it (which is surprisingly difficult, by the way). Some consider it an emotion, while others consider it a trait. There are still others who prefer to define gratitude in terms of behavior. Others have labeled it a virtue, a personal disposition, or even a skill. For our purposes here, we'll adopt the definition of one of the world's leading experts on the science of gratitude, Dr. Robert Emmons from University of California at Davis. He defines gratitude as having two essential elements. The first is "an affirmation of goodness" where we recognize a blessing or a positive outcome. The second aspect is identifying where that goodness comes from.

When we take the time to affirm what is good in our lives and then recognize the source of that goodness, there is an amazing impact on overall health and resiliency. Consider just some of what we know about the power of gratitude:

◆ Focusing on gratitude stimulates the hypothalamus in the brain (which helps to regulate stress) and the ventral tegmental (part of the brain's reward and pleasure system). In other words, gratitude helps you manage stress and makes you feel better (Zahn et al., 2009).

◆ Individuals who express gratitude are less vulnerable to mood swings and are generally less moody (McCullough et al., 2004).

◆ When compared to times of stress, worry, and anxiety, the brain is more efficient and reflective when we are grateful (Amen and Amen, 2016).

◆ Grateful people are physically healthier and sleep better (Emmons and McCullough, 2003).

◆ Demonstrating gratitude reduces negative emotions and aggression (DeWall, 2012).

◆ Gratitude can help with self-control and resisting temptation (DeSteno et al., 2014).

◆ Expressing gratitude, even in the small things, reduces stress and builds resiliency (Seligman and Steen, 2005).

◆ When we express thankfulness and gratitude to someone, they are more likely to help us in the future (Grant and Gino, 2010).

For a deeper dive into the research, check out the white paper published by The Greater Good Science Center out of UC Berkeley titled *The Science of Gratitude* (2018). In essence, gratitude serves as an "amplifier of good", as Dr. Emmons describes it, and acts as a buffer during stressful times.

To build resiliency in order to manage stress, we start by practicing gratitude. Lots and lots of it. Gratitude isn't about ignoring the challenges in life, it's about recognizing the blessings. It's about taking time to realize that there are good things in life – specific things – that surround us on a daily basis. Even in the midst of significant headwinds, blessings are all around us.

Recall that resiliency consists of two things: how we think and what we do. It consists of our thinking patterns as well as the specific coping mechanisms we employ during challenging times. Gratitude helps with both; when we take time to count our blessings and we take specific steps to express our appreciation, we are practicing resilience.

Application Points

- ◆ *Don't wait* – Expressing thankfulness, appreciation, and gratitude shouldn't be something we save for Thanksgiving dinner or the Kumbaya campfire moments when we are away at a retreat. Make it a regular habit.
- ◆ *Pay it forward* – Do good for others without an expectation that the deeds be reciprocated. Better yet, do them anonymously.
- ◆ *Keep a gratitude journal* – Writing for as little as a few minutes per day goes a long way in helping to reduce stress (O'Connell et al., 2017). For those of you who may not be inclined to do free-form journaling, simply create a bulleted list of the things that went well on any given day. Think of big things (e.g. a student who struggles with self-control had a great day) and small things that often go unnoticed (e.g. the custodial staff did a great job of cleaning the classroom).
- ◆ *Write a thank you note* – Good old-fashioned handwritten thank you notes, while they may be a lost art, go a long way in helping to express gratitude, and they serve as a great method to encourage and support others. Write notes to colleagues, students, parents, friends, family, and even to administrators.
- ◆ *Write a letter* – Letters are typically more in-depth and they certainly take more time. But the process of writing a letter forces us to be thoughtful and reflective, thus supporting a mindset of resiliency.

◆ *Send an email* – When we've only got a few minutes, a quick email expressing appreciation is powerful. Text messages serve a similar purpose – quick and easy ways to say "thank you".

◆ *Make a phone call* – Few things are better than a good ol' fashioned phone call. When people hear our voice, they can sense our tone, genuineness, and our heart-felt appreciation.

◆ *Make a list* – At the end of the day, make a list of a few good things that happened throughout the day. One study found that this simple exercise helped to manage stress, increase happiness, and foster hope (Fleming, 2006).

◆ *Create G.O. moments with students* – Friend and fellow educator LeAnn Nickelsen encourages us to create gratitude and optimism moments with students. They could be as simple as journaling opportunities, teachable moments when there is an unexpected surprise, or planned discussion questions related to the content.

◆ *Teach students how to express gratitude* – Students can do any of the above strategies – they could write a thank you note or pay it forward, but there are also specific things you can do in the classroom. Try some of these: 3 Things Thursdays (or a variation) where students simply list or discuss three things that they are appreciative for; "Bucket Fillers" or similar activities where students write notes of appreciation for specific things and give those notes to their peers; pictures or videos of people expressing appreciation; using the letters A-Z students to brainstorm specific things they appreciate; or share books, articles, or stories where appreciation and thankfulness are central themes.

3

Resilient Teachers Practice Reframing

In a nutshell: As a form of positive self-talk, reframing is a technique where we consciously choose to change the way we think about a situation in front of us. It is a way to balance our thinking in order to gain perspective and control.

Digging Deeper: Sometimes referred to as cognitive restructuring, cognitive re-appraisal, or simply positive self-talk, reframing is a thinking tool that empowers us to find alternatives to a situation we are currently facing. Basically, reframing is about choosing to view something from a different perspective. Much like a frame around a painting can influence the way we view the art, reframing is a powerful resiliency tool because it gives us a specific coping mechanism that helps us to take control by changing our thinking.

Years ago, I got stuck in San Francisco traffic. Really horrendous traffic. If you've never experienced traffic jams in the Bay Area, add that to your gratitude list. Finding myself getting frustrated at the lack of progress (and the confusing lay out of streets and freeways in the Bay Area), I started to grumble and get frustrated. I wasn't pounding the steering wheel in anger, mind you. But I was annoyed and the charm of a beautiful city was quickly wearing off.

As my frustration grew, so did my stress levels. Recall that the stress response kicks in when you feel like you have no control. Traffic in San Francisco is the definition of no control. In the midst of that traffic-induced frustration, I elected to reframe the experience. I chose to look at my current situation from a different perspective. That's all reframing is – choosing to view a situation, a relationship, an environment, or a context from a different point of view. While it's not necessarily easy, it's extremely powerful.

So, I said to myself, "At least you get to spend some more time in this brand new rental car. When you get home, you have to drive a 7-year-old Honda that is overdue for an oil change and a tire rotation. And, at the end of the day you don't have to get this car washed." That was my reframe; my self-talk and internal dialogue was changed. Instead of choosing to remain frustrated, I did my best to find something positive in the situation.

Reframing is all about being mindful of our thinking patterns and choosing to look at something differently. As I thought about the traffic differently, I took some control. As my control increased, my stress levels (and irritation) decreased. Remember that resilience consists of two things: how we think and what we do. It consists of our thinking patterns (including that voice inside our heads that we talk to) and the coping mechanisms we use when things begin to be challenging. In essence, reframing give us the control we need to change our thinking and move forward. It helps to get us unstuck.

Reframing is a form of *Positive Self-talk*. The truth is that we all talk to ourselves. Some of us, depending on our backgrounds and experiences, have pretty positive, uplifting, and encouraging conversations in our heads. Some of us have the opposite. Choosing to control those negative, intrusive voices is part of being resilient.

When I told myself that the traffic delay was an opportunity to enjoy a new car, it changed the way I thought about the situation. Notice that I didn't paint a false picture that it was a great experience or that I was lucky to get caught in traffic. I didn't tell myself that it was equivalent to a pleasant stroll along the beach. But I changed the narrative and chose to find the silver lining.

In school settings, when we practice the art of reframing, we begin to view challenging students, difficult colleagues, un-communicative leadership, or inadequate resources differently. Although a bit cliché-ish, reframing is telling yourself that the cup is indeed half-full. It's not actually changing the situation; it's merely choosing to focus on the positives of the experience.

Dr. Steven Wolin, an expert on the development of resilience and director of Project Resilience, contends that reframing is central to the development of resilience. Resilience is not about ignoring or downplaying the challenges in front of us (or the past traumas we are overcoming), it's about looking at them differently. Reframing is especially important as we strive to meet the needs of students who may have behavioral and/or learning difficulties.

In full disclosure, reframing is not always easy. It takes effort (and some mental gymnastics) to find the positive in the midst of an ugly or uncomfortable state of affairs. And, it takes practice. But there is evidence, specifically in education, that reframing as a form of mindfulness helps to reduce stress and teacher burnout (Flook et al., 2013).

Application Points

◆ *Follow three steps*: *Realize – Label – Choose:* Start by simply realizing or acknowledging the stressor you are facing. Follow by labeling or identifying the stressor. For example, if you are irritated at something, say, "This has me irritated". Then, choose to reframe the situation by changing the way you think about it.

◆ *Go from "have to" to "get to"* – When you think of some of the duties and tasks that you are responsible for, adopt the mindset of "*I get to…*" rather than "*I have to…*". For example, you may need to return a phone call to a parent that you anticipate will be challenging. Rather than say, "*I have to call this parent*", say to yourself, "*I get to call this parent*". That one small change may be enough to shift thinking in order to see the phone call as an opportunity rather than an obligation. Plus, when we view things as opportunities, we are much less likely to procrastinate or avoid them all together.

◆ *Repeat power phrases* – Say things like, *"Nothing lasts forever"* and *"This too shall pass"*. A variation of those statements is the question, *"Will this matter in 1 week?"* Much of the time, the answer is, *"No, not really"*. Why get upset, bothered, or stressed out about things that, in the big scheme of life, don't matter all that much and probably won't even be remembered.

◆ *Remember your strengths* – Follow the advice of Psychologist Edith Grotberg who tells us that sometimes we need to be reminded of our own strengths, assets, and resources. She encourages people to regularly remind themselves of three things by simply responding to the sentence starters "I have…", "I can…", and "I am…"

◆ *List a child's strengths* – Take a moment and think about a student who is currently struggling in your class. They might be struggling because of an academic gap or they might be demonstrating negative or unproductive behaviors. List that child's strengths. Is that child passionate? Caring? Do they have great attendance? Do they stick up for their friends? Are they an athlete or cook or artist or dancer? When we begin to view others as unique individuals with discernable strengths, we can begin to reframe our interactions with them.

◆ *Share those strengths* – After you've made a list of a student's strengths, share it with that student and their family. Tell the child all the good you see in them. Tell the parents as well. The simple act of identifying and communicating those strengths will do wonders for both you and the student.

◆ *Reframe student behavior* – When we are frustrated by student behavior, it can be easy to get stuck in a negative mindset and, as a result, use less-than-productive descriptions to label student behaviors. Instead, consider the positive correlates to negative labels we place on kids.

For example, a "stubborn" student could be viewed as determined. A rebellious student might be labeled an independent one and a profane student could be viewed as expressive. When we elect to think about a student as expressive and opinionated rather than rude and disrespectful, it often changes the way we feel about a child. When we reframe negative student behavior, it opens the door to opportunities and appreciation.

4

Resilient Teachers Understand the Power of "No"

In a Nutshell: Saying yes to too many things increases your stress levels. Learning when to say no (and what to say no to) helps you to manage stress.

Digging Deeper: To begin, consider what Warren Buffet describes as one essential tool for success – really successful people say no to almost everything. Why is that? How might saying yes to fewer things actually lead to greater levels of resilience and greater levels of satisfaction with your job?

First, let's acknowledge that it is not always easy to say no. Many of us genuinely want to help where and when we can. Sometimes, guilt kicks in when we say no to someone (and feeling guilty stinks). Sometimes, it's hard to say no to people that we truly care about. It's important to understand that saying no to things makes sense on a rational level, but it's not always easy to do. In fact, for some of us, it's downright tough. It's a simple idea that can be really hard to put into practice. But keep reading, I'll show you some simple steps to make it easier.

Second, many of us battle with FOMO – *the fear of missing out*. When we say no to something, it necessarily means that we'll miss out on it. Sometimes, the experience we'll miss could be filled with fun things that we really want to do. Ugh – that's often a difficult choice. Saying yes to something could result in an amazing experience. But, saying yes might also mean that there is less time to do other things that are more important for long-term health, happiness, satisfaction, and job effectiveness. Dan Triarico, author of *The Zen Teacher* (2015), puts it bluntly, "… trying to be the master of all things puts you on the A-train directly to Burnout Land".

Considering whether to say yes or no to additional responsibilities is a cost-benefit analysis. I have to weigh the potential benefits against what it's going to cost me. I have to answer the question, *"If I give up my time, energy, and focus (and sometimes my money) to do this will it be worth it when I weigh those benefits against what I'll lose?" If I say yes to something like sponsoring an after-school club for my students, will that mean that I have less time for planning and grading? If I say yes to serving on a civic board or committee, will that negatively impact the time I have for my family? If I say yes to starting a master's program, will I still be able to _____ ".* You get the point – we must be business-like in our thinking about whether or not to take on additional responsibilities.

Here is why we need to carefully consider what we say "yes" to – taking on too many responsibilities increases stress levels. When I am proficiently handling all the things on my "plate" (when I am handling things well, that is), my stress levels are typically reasonable and manageable. When I take on too many things (when I say yes to way too much), you guessed it – I get stressed out. And, when I'm stressed out, I don't do *anything* nearly as well. A juggling analogy works here. If I can proficiently juggle three balls, and I'm only asked to juggle three, things are peachy. If I can only juggle three, and a fourth ball is thrown in the mix, I drop them all. And when I drop things (when I'm no longer as effective as I once was), I get stressed out, I feel guilty, and I start to doubt my calling as an educator. Or I may simply get burned out and consider looking for another occupation. That's all very stressful.

Application Points

◆ *When someone asks you to consider taking on a responsibility, you don't have to answer immediately.* Take time to consider your response. Simply say something like, "Thanks for asking. I appreciate that you thought of me. Let me think about it and I'll let you know in a day or two". In other words, don't feel pressured to give an immediate response. Notice that I didn't suggest that you say, "Could I let you know in a day or two?" We don't need to ask permission to take time to be thoughtful and reflective. If someone pressures you for an immediate yes or no, you may regret your decision. You may say yes out of guilt but that may result in you being less-than-committed to the outcome. We all know what happens when we only do something out of guilt or obligation. We are not typically at our very best under those conditions.

♦ *When you decide to say yes or no, communicate that decision quickly.* This is especially important if you have to say no to someone. In other words, don't drag it out and procrastinate. Why? The more you procrastinate (especially if you feel like the other person is going to be disappointed with you), the more you'll ruminate and worry about their response. Rumination and worry = stress. Get it over with quickly. Rip off that band aide in one swift and purposeful motion.

♦ *Don't feel obligated to give a reason for every decision.* Consider what E.B. White (the guy who wrote *Charlotte's Web*) once said when asked to serve on a committee promoting the arts and sciences: "I must decline, for secret reasons". Yes, people often want to know why you declined but don't feel pressured to justify every decision. You're a grownup who does not have to rationalize everything to everyone. Period. Simply decline in a polite and respectful way by saying something like, "Thanks for asking. I appreciate that you thought of me but at this time I need to say no". Notice that there is something missing in that previous statement. It starts with the letter *a*. When I decline something, I don't feel the need to apologize. I didn't say, "I am so sorry but I won't be able to participate this time around". Not only did I not apologize, I didn't provide a rationale or an explanation. I realize that this may sound cold or impersonal. That's not the point. In fact, when

I have to decline something, I always do so in a direct, kind, and respectful way. And, too much information may simply burden the other person and make them feel guilty for asking. The fact is that you want people to ask you to take on responsibilities. It's good when people ask things of you. It shows that they trust you and believe that you are capable of doing good things. If you provide a lengthy, apology-ridden response, the other person may think "Geez, I'm sorry I asked". What happens in that case? Both of you are likely to feel guilty (which results in increased stress).

◆ *Offer alternatives.* If you genuinely want to help with something but are unable to assist in the specific way you've been asked, suggest alternatives. Say something like, "Thanks for thinking of me. This sounds like an amazing opportunity. I'm unable to commit to doing _____, but I could _____". This shows that you are still interested and it may offer suggestions that the other person hadn't considered. For example, you may say, "I'd be thrilled to run the after-school robotics club but I can't commit to 3 days per week. If you could find me a partner to split the duties, I'm in". Notice again, what is missing from that last statement. There is no question; you are not asking if it would be possible to find a partner. You are also not taking on the responsibility to find yourself a partner. This is an example of advocating for yourself in a very concrete and direct way.

◆ *Ask for specifics.* When you are considering how to respond to a request – when doing your cost-benefit analysis – ask for specifics. Before you say yes, make sure you have all the facts. Ask about the time commitment. Ask about financial obligations. Ask about leadership. Ask about who else will be involved. Those last two questions are of utmost importance. The additional responsibility might be something that you'd like to do and that you have the capacity to do well, but if it is being led by or consisting of people that you don't have full trust in, there will be problems. And, when you are in a situation where you are surrounded by people that you don't fully trust (or people that you don't really like all that much), you are likely not to give it your best effort. When you are in a situation where you are surrounded by people you don't enjoy spending time with, your stress increases. You see the theme, right? Saying "no" is a great way to build your resilience by managing stress.

◆ *When it comes to the time commitment, double it.* If the person says, "This committee only meets once per month for about an hour", I'm going to count on it being much more than just an hour a month. The fact is that some people are just plain bad at estimating how much time it takes for someone else to do something. The other person is not necessarily being dishonest, it's just really hard to esti-mate accurately how much time it will take for someone else to get something done. It is especially important to double that estimate when you are first doing something. If you over-estimate and it doesn't take as much time as you estimated – bonus! You are better off if you mentally and emotionally over-estimate something (it will take three hours, and it only takes two) than if you underesti-mate and it takes more time than you planned for.

◆ *Consider the request and the requestor.* The fact is that not all requests or requestors are created equally. A request from distant cousin to help him move into a new house over the weekend is not given the same level of consid-eration as a request that comes from my supervisor. Even though I don't feel the need to justify every decision to every person, there are some situations where I dig a bit deeper. There are some people that I give a bit more thought and credibility to. For example, if your principal comes to you and says, "I'd like you to consider leading Parent Teacher Organization (PTO) meetings for the next semester. I know you have your sights on being in a lead-ership position in the near future and this experience will really help". That request (and the requestor) is elevated in my thinking. In those cases, I then ask myself, "Do I need to take anything off my plate so that I could do this really well?"

One last idea – I know that many of you are people-pleasers. You hate the idea of disappointing someone. It tears you up inside to think that someone might not be pleased with a decision that you make. I get it. I'd rather live with people-pleasers than people-haters. But you might need to fight your instincts on this one. Plus, it's good to remind yourself that the people in your life who truly love you – those who truly "have your back" – will still love you, even if you say no to them. Those that don't truly care about you aren't likely to be satisfied even if you say yes.

OK, one *more* last idea. The former school principal and central-office administrator in me feels compelled to clarify that there are some things that we can't say no to. There are things you were hired to do; things you don't have a choice to do. For example, if your school or district has adopted a new reading curriculum, you can't say, "Well, Dr. Harris suggested that I say yes to fewer responsibilities in order to better manage my stress levels so I'm going to politely decline to implement the new curriculum". If you do that, we'll both be in hot water. Rather, it's better to start with those non-negotiable responsibilities and make sure we are doing those things well before we add on too many additional non-required responsibilities.

5

Resilient Teachers Manage Their Emotions

In a Nutshell: To be human is to experience emotions, both positive and negative. As educators, we are bombarded with a flood of emotions on a daily basis. Understanding the role of emotions and how to manage negative emotional situations is a must in order to be resilient.

Digging Deeper: First, notice that the title of this chapter is not "*Resilient Teachers Control their Emotions*". Emotions cannot be controlled, they just happen. As a built-in survival mechanism, emotions play an essential role in our daily lives. Without going in to a long research-heavy discussion on the role of emotions in the brain, let's work from this premise: Emotions serve as a tool for your brain to help determine things like safety and security along with helping to determine what gets focused attention as well as what gets remembered (Tyng et al., 2017).

Some serious researchers and heavy hitters have done intensive studies looking at the role of emotions in the brain. Probably the best known is Daniel Goleman, who, in 1995, published the first edition of his best-selling book titled *Emotional Intelligence*. In it, he challenged us to consider that emotional intelligence is as important as traditional measures of intelligence. The good news is that emotional intelligence can be taught, cultivated, and improved over time. Sometimes referred to as EQ (emotional quotient), the idea is that an individual's ability to reflect upon and appropriately express emotions is a better predictor of success in life than traditional measures, such as IQ.

It is impossible to discuss the concept of resilience without delving into emotions. In fact, many researchers don't simply refer to resilience as a stand-alone concept; they refer to *emotional resilience*. This makes sense because stressful events almost always include a negative emotional reaction. People who are resilient understand that the expression of positive emotions is a powerful coping mechanism that helps them to overcome negative emotional experiences (Tugade and Fredrickson, 2004).

James Gross, from the Stanford University Psychophysiology Lab, has looked into the connection between emotional regulation and resilience. He suggests that people who acknowledge their emotions (both positive and negative) and deal with those emotions in productive ways tend to be more resilient than those who do not (Gross and John, 2003).

When we do not deal with our emotions in productive ways, it can result in what experts call *somatization of emotions*. This is when we experience physical problems resulting from undealt with negative emotions. Those physical problems range from stomach problems to general aches and pains and even hair loss (Abbass, 2005). In essence, there is a physiology to our emotions and when we don't address negative emotions in a positive manner, it is bound to show up somewhere in our body.

At this point, you might be saying something like *"Hold on, Bryan. Didn't you say that stress and control are related? Shouldn't I try to control my emotions in order to lower my stress? I thought control was a good thing"*. If you thought something like that, you have a good point. Let's discuss the nuance between control and manage. You are right – control is a good thing. The reason we use the term *manage* here is that emotions cannot really be controlled. They just seem to happen. Emotions are a survival mechanism in the brain designed to respond rapidly to any perceived threat. Acting a bit like a smoke detector, the amygdala (the part of your brain primarily responsible for processing emotions) sends out an alarm when it detects a threat. This super-fast reaction is involuntary and automatic. And you guessed it – it cannot be controlled. You cannot, for example, control whether or not you feel fear when being verbally attached. What you can control is your thinking patterns and your responses once you realize that you are fearful.

Application Points

♦ *Avoiding negative emotions rarely helps.* You might be able to detour around them for a while but they almost always come back. Our goal is not to live a life free of negative emotions, our goal is to find powerful and effective ways to respond when faced with them.

♦ *Recognize that emotions are just things.* And they are fleeting things at that. Negative emotions are merely clues that something in your life needs attention. It is not good or bad to have negative emotions, it's just a clue that something is amiss and needs to addressed. The power and control you have is in how you respond.

♦ *Label the emotion.* Since ignoring negative emotions is futile, you are better off using emotions, both positive and negative, in productive ways. Pioneers in the study of emotional intelligence John Mayer and Peter Salovey (1997) suggest that emotionally intelligent people do four things: they perceive the emotions of others, they perceive their own emotions, they use emotions as a thinking and decision-making tool, and they regulate their emotions.

♦ *Then take action.* Once you have labeled an emotion (frustrated, irritable, confused, annoyed, guilt-ridden), take control by doing something that you know will boost your mood: go for a walk, practice some gratitude, or seek support from a trusted colleague.

♦ *Review the ideas and suggestions listed in the Reframing chapter.* Often referred to as re-appraisal, when we choose to look at a negative situation from a different perspective, it can provide a sense of control and help us to put the situation into perspective.

♦ Ask yourself to "Just Imagine". In his super-practical book titled *Exactly What to Say - The Magic Words for Influence and Impact,* author Phil Jones says that these two simple but powerful words have a unique way of influencing thought. The idea here is that we gain some control over our thinking and emotions by imaging a different emotion or a different outcome. It might go like this: "Imagine what it will feel like in three weeks when this situation has passed" or "Just imagine the relief you'll feel when …"

◆ *Place limits.* Specifically, place limits on those things you know are likely to spur negative emotional reactions. For example, while you might love to follow politics, consuming hours of talk radio or cable news every day might not be the healthiest thing to do. Or, while you might love to stay up to date with friends and family on social media, constantly peering in to the lives of others is bound to make you dissatisfied with your life due to constant comparisons.

◆ *Make time for positive emotions.* Resilience is sometimes described as an individual's "self-righting" process. There are simply times when we need to realize that things are not right. We need to take command and "right the ship". A great way to do that is to carve out time on a consistent basis to do those things that are likely to produce positive emotions. Sprinkled throughout this book are tons of ways to make that happen. Examples include: expressing gratitude, having fun with your students, getting things checked off your to-do list, accomplishing goals, and developing supportive professional relationships.

6

Resilient Teachers Know Their Triggers

In a Nutshell: A "trigger" is a situation, person, context, memory, or anything that produces a negative emotional reaction and causes us to revert to a fixed mindset. Carol Dweck (2016) calls them "the battle within us all". Being aware of those situations that produce a less-than-productive emotional response is an essential resiliency skill.

Digging Deeper: In the previous chapter, we discussed the importance of managing emotions. Here, we'll go just a bit deeper into one very specific thing that impacts us as educators – there are certain things that just tick us off, push our buttons, or drive us crazy. We'll call those our triggers – things that cause us to revert to poor behaviors or negative thinking patterns.

Recall that the role of emotions in our lives is centered on survival. When we are "triggered", all it really means is that we have an immediate negative emotional reaction to some sort of threat. That immediate negative reaction is a defense mechanism designed to protect you by rejecting the situation, counter attacking, or withdrawing. Sigmund Freud, everyone's favorite controversial psychoanalyst, talked about defense mechanisms all the way back in the 1800s. Put simply, when we are triggered by something, we go into defense mode in order to protect ourselves.

Sheila Heen and Douglas Stone, in their article published in Harvard's small but powerful book, simply titled *Resilience* (2017), reminds us that the goal is not to avoid or pretend that triggers don't exist. Rather the goal is to acknowledge them and use them as a tool for growth and self-reflection. To make things more challenging, most of us are unaware of our thinking patterns and coping mechanisms when we're under stress (Margolis and Stoltz, 2018). That is, we have a way of responding – a set of thinking patterns and habits – that we don't always think carefully through. Far too many of us are reactive, not responsive when it comes to life's challenges. As a result, we often just "go with our gut". While this works sometimes, part of the job of becoming more resilient is coming to understand yourself better.

While we are on the topic of better understanding ourselves, let's talk about a significant challenge we face as teachers – dealing with student behavior (specifically, dealing with student *misbehavior*). The truth is that many of us are triggered by the behavior of our students. One of the reasons it is so important to cultivate your own resiliency is that there will be times when student misbehaviors trigger a negative emotional reaction in you.

It's OK, we can admit it. There are simply times when students drive us nuts. Acknowledging the fact that some behaviors get under your skin is not a weakness. In fact, the better you know yourself and what triggers you, the better you'll be at responding in positive ways. If we don't acknowledge and seek to understand our own pet peeves and irritations, we could become part of the problem. Susan Craig, in the book *Trauma-Sensitive Schools* (2016), speaks to the importance of having good coping mechanisms because they help us to maintain professional objectivity. Otherwise, she points out, we may fall victim to personalizing student behavior. If we do that – if we become personally offended – we then become part of the problem.

As a quick experiment, take a moment to consider which types of student misbehaviors most bother you. The list below, while not exhaustive, is a good place to start. Which of the following behaviors most get to you?

- In-attention or lack of focus
- Side talking or blurting out
- Having to repeat directions
- Using cell phones without permission
- Cheating
- Tardiness
- Messiness
- Stalling or wasting time
- Off task questions ("Can I go to the bathroom?")
- Excessive physical movement
- Tattling
- Crying
- Perfectionism
- Rude or disrespectful comments
- Profanity
- Bullying

The goal of this self-reflection activity is to simply acknowledge those behaviors that are likely to trigger an emotional response. For example, if you were bullied as a child, you might be hyper-sensitive to situations that look like bullying. If so, if that is a trigger of yours, you might not have the objectivity necessary to help students. The better we know ourselves, the better we can be prepared with an appropriate response when triggered. Again, the goal is not to pretend that nothing gets to you. We are all human and there will be things that irritate the heck out of us. The goal is to acknowledge, take control, and use specific coping mechanisms *when* you are triggered.

Application Points

- *Reframe* – Refer back to the list of student behaviors you just reviewed, and then go back and review the chapter on the power of reframing. How might you look at those specific behaviors differently? For example, if student messiness gets to you, could that be a sign of a creative student?
- *Differentiate between "what" and "who"* – There are times when we are triggered by people; there are times when

we are triggered by events. Resilient people are able to identify the source of the trigger and not inappropriately confound the two (Sheen and Stone, 2017).

◆ *Recognize ANTs* – Daniel and Tana Amen, in their book *The Brain Warrior's Way* (2016), define ANTs as *automatic negative thoughts*. We all have those moments where strange, inappropriate, or negative thoughts enter our minds. Just because we have a thought, doesn't make it true nor does it mean we have to entertain it. The Amens remind us that, "Thoughts lie; they lie a lot, and it is our unquestioned or uninvestigated thoughts that steal our happiness. Having a thought has nothing to do with whether or not it is true…" One strategy they suggest to deal with ANTs is to write them down and ask yourself questions about them.

◆ *Recognize fatigue* – Classrooms are places that demand a lot of energy. Emotional energy, physical energy, spiritual energy – it can be exhausting! So, simply recognize that the more tired you get, the easier it is to be triggered by something that you might be able to ignore when you have plenty of energy.

◆ *Use the "Golden Rule of Triggers"* – Tony Schwartz, writing for the Harvard Business Review, describes the Golden Rule this way – Whatever you feel compelled to do when you are experiencing that negative emotion, don't do it. If you feel like lashing out, yelling, pounding something, or doing something that you know won't help the situation, "hold your fire".

◆ *Be honest* – The truth is that the people around you, especially your students, probably already know what your triggers are. The good news is that nobody expects perfection. When you are able to extend grace and understanding when kids have a bad day, they are more likely to reciprocate when you have one.

◆ *Practice in-the-moment stress relievers* – Take a look at the next chapter for strategies and coping mechanism that are immediately helpful for managing those negative emotions that arise from a triggering event.

7

Resilient Teachers Practice In-The-Moment Stress Relievers

In a Nutshell: Let's be honest, there are simply times when we get overwhelmed, annoyed, and ticked off. Because we can't always be a "super hero" educator, we need to have some tools and strategies that we can implement when we sense our stress levels increasing.

Digging Deeper: In the previous two chapters, we looked at the importance of managing emotions and we considered how triggering events can sometimes bring out the worst in us. And, we've established that stress is the brain and body's response to a perception of a lack of control over something (typically negative or threatening) happening in our life. That phrase "lack of control" is practically synonymous with being a teacher. Make no mistake, there is much that is within our control (more about that in Chapter 11), but the fact is that every day can bring unique and sometimes-unexpected challenges.

Let's take a moment and dig just a little deeper into *how* stress typically manifests itself. Recall that what we label as stress is merely the brain and body's response to a threat. That response, depending on the strength of the perceived threat, happens very quickly, and we sometimes don't consciously realize what is happening. We just know that we feel tense, irritable, or cautious.

So, the first thing we need to realize is the fact that we may not be consciously aware of our increasing stress levels. As a result, we need to pay attention to our bodies. Often our bodies will tell us we are stressed before we consciously realize it. Why is this the case? The brain and body's stress response is designed to help you tackle challenges; traditionally, those challenges are physical in nature. Among other things, the release of cortisol in the system rushes blood flow to your core muscles (abdomen, thighs, legs) in order to equip you to address that perceived threat (Sapolsky, 2004). You've heard of the brain's *fight, flight, or freeze* mechanism. It's rooted in this idea: when you feel stress as a result of a perceived threat, your brain and body responds by giving you the physical and mental resources necessary to address that threat.

Paying attention to our bodies is a great way to take stock of our stress levels. For some of us, we feel tension in our muscles (for me, I feel the muscles in my mid-back start to tighten up). Some of us get jittery, sweaty, or "edgy". While we may just chalk these feelings up to fatigue, tiredness, or just having an off day, it may be your body telling you that something is out of whack.

Now, let's consider what to do when we sense the stressors are getting the best of us. Whether we are triggered by a certain event or we feel stress because of the cumulative effects of lots of factors, it is good to have a toolbox of ready-to-go coping strategies that help us to gain some control and perspective. Below are examples of "real-time resilience" as Reivich and Shatte (2002) describe it. These are calming and focusing techniques that help to bring perspective and proper thinking in the midst of stressful situations.

Application Points

◆ *Breathe* – As silly as it may sound, just breathe. Take some deep breaths and get some fresh oxygen into the system. When kids are having a meltdown or having a difficult time regulating their behavior, what do we tell them to do? Breathe. It does wonders.

◆ *Move your body* – Stress is a physical thing, it's not just happening in our brains. Perceived threat increases levels of cortisol and adrenaline; those chemicals want to take action. So, do something physical in order to mediate that stress. Go for a walk, dance, watch some GoNoodle videos with your students, play Simon Says, etc. The worst thing we can do is to stay sedentary or motionless when you are feeling stressed.

◆ *Practice reframing* – This suggestion seems to keep popping up over and over. That's because it is powerful and effective. As a form of self-talk, reframing is the practice of choosing to think differently about a challenge or problem in front of us. While it's not always simple, I can choose to control the way I think about a situation. Deal with stress by gaining back some control; one way to start is with the way you think.

◆ *Externalize information* – Sometimes, the imbalance we feel results from a sense that we have too much to do and not enough time to get it done. Whether it's tackling a pile of papers that need to be graded or taking care of things at home, making a to-do list or a checklist is a great way to gain some sense of control. When we externalize all the tasks that need to be done, it allows us to organize and prioritize. Essentially, gain some control by breaking things down into smaller pieces. After all, when kids get overwhelmed by big tasks, we "chunk" things for them. It can work wonders for us as well.

◆ *Make social connections* – Reach out to those people in your life who are able to provide clarity, support, words of encouragement, and (perhaps) a kick in the pants. Sometimes, we need a hug; sometimes, we need encouragement; and sometimes, we just need to see a friendly face. The truth is that positive relationships serve as the foundation for overcoming challenges. Building and practicing resilience is a team sport. Simon Sinek, the guy who wrote the hugely popular book *Start with Why*, stated it perfectly in a Tweet when he said, "Relationships matter. It is those around us that have the power to inspire us to keep going. On the days we want to give up, they are the ones that say "We need this. We need you. Keep going".

- *Talk to yourself* – Repeat things like, "This too shall pass" or ask yourself, "What's the worst thing that could happen?" One of the good things about emotions is that they rarely last for very long. The good news is that by taking some specific steps, we can reduce the amount of time that a negative emotion has its hooks in us.
- *Do something fun* – Have a good laugh, smile at some old yearbook pictures, play a game, tell knock-knock jokes, or do a silly dance. Don't wallow, take control. Instead of assuming that your emotions always have control over you, turn the tables and do something concrete to change how you feel.

8

Resilient Teachers Develop a Professional Support Network

In a Nutshell: Because teaching is stressful at times, we all need a network of mentors, colleagues, and friends who can help us navigate the waters during good and bad times. Success is rarely achieved yourself.

Digging Deeper: Whether we want to admit it or not, other people have a tremendous influence on us. Although we like to think of ourselves as independent thinkers who have the ability and fortitude to follow our own path, the fact is that the people who surround us do have an influence. Sometimes, that influence is subtle and flies under the radar; other times, it's more obvious. This is not to assume that we are all sheep who blindly follow, but who we spend time with influences our thinking and behavior. Be thoughtful about who you let into life. The right people will make you better. The wrong people will make you miserable.

Resilient teachers are proactive about building and sustaining supportive relationships with their colleagues. They develop a network of people who help them to manage the stressors of the job. Among other things, having a positive network of mentors, colleagues, and friends: strengthens our immune system and helps to improve our overall physical health (Sapolsky, 2004); improves job satisfaction (Mansfield et al., 2014); increases the likelihood that we'll continue in the profession (Harris, 2015);

helps us to manage stress (Hartling, 2008); and, perhaps most importantly, good relationships result in longer life (Holt-Lunstad et al., 2010).

Some people, when they hear the advice to "build relationships", immediately think of touchy-feely activities that are centered on the sharing of feelings and emotions. If you lean that way, consider this: the United States military has a program called "Comprehensive Soldier Fitness" that includes a component called "Master Resilience Training" designed especially for drill sergeants. Now, most of us wouldn't assume that drill sergeants are the model of positive relationships. But one of the five foundational principles to this training is an understanding of the role of relationships in building resilience.

If you are looking for even more evidence of the power and importance of positive relationships, here is the cherry on top of the research sundae. In a pair of longitudinal studies going all the way back to the 1930s, researchers at Harvard tracked the physical, emotional, and relational health of groups of men for decades. Referred to as the Grant and Glueck studies, combined they collected 80 years' worth of data that consistently point to one finding – long, healthy, and happy lives require social bonds and positive relationships.

A note about mentors and coaches – we need them because it is very difficult to get better on our own. Is it impossible? No, of course not. But think about it this way, why do the very best athletes in the world need coaches? In fact, top-level athletes are often coached, guided, and led by people who were never nearly as good as they are. Take, for example, the NFL's best-ever quarter back. Many people would say Tom Brady is the GOAT (greatest of all time). Brady is a better quarterback than any single person who ever coached him. I'll make this argument – Brady is the GOAT *because* he was coached. It's not a sign of weakness to be coached; it's a sign of arrogance to assume that no coach is needed. To be the very best version of yourself, you need others to push, pull, praise, guide, question, and gently correct you when your thinking or actions are wrong.

If it's true that the people around us influence our thinking and behavior patterns, we do well to surround ourselves with people who are good for us. After all, isn't that what we tell kids – *be careful about who you hang out with because you'll start to behave like them*. So, seek out positive colleagues who are enthusiastic about the profession. The sad truth is that every campus has some teachers who are already burned out and some who are getting pretty crispy around the edges. The positive truth is that every campus also has teachers who love what they do, find meaning and purpose in their work, and fulfillment in their jobs. Seek out those people. It may require that you venture down the hall or engage with colleagues in a different grade level or department, but they're out there. Go find them.

Application Points

- ◆ *Avoid isolation* – Sometimes when things are tough, we want to close the doors, lock ourselves away, and wait for the storm to pass. While this might seem intuitive, it's one of the worse things we can do.
- ◆ *Ask for help* – Remember to seek help when you need it. It's not a sign of weakness to seek assistance; it's a sign of weakness not to. After all, we expect our students to seek help when they need it, right? It's not a sign of weakness to say, "Hey, things are piling up. I could use an extra hand".
- ◆ *Celebrate* – Part of building positive relationships is celebrating a person's successes or milestones. Celebrate your own, those of your students, and those of your colleagues and school.
- ◆ *Share a meal* – Eat lunch at least once per week with a peer and don't talk about school. Also, once a month, share a meal with an older person. It doesn't matter if they have similar background or not. It doesn't matter if they've never been a classroom teacher. Just soak up their wisdom and perspective. Ask questions, seek advice.
- ◆ *Give support* – Keep an eye out for ways you can help others. It turns out that giving support to others is a win-win. Not only does the other person benefit from your generosity, helping others reduces your own stress

(Orehek and Inagaki, 2017). Specifically, remember to reach out to newer staff members.

◆ *Build, Maintain, Restore* – Relationships need to be "strategically managed". That's the way Ronald Culbertson – author of *Do it Well Make it Fun* – puts it. To remain resilient, focus on building positive relationships along with remembering to maintain existing ones. There will also be times when you need to restore a relationship that may have been damaged.

◆ *Get a mentor* – They help as a sounding board during stressful times. When you are stressed, you don't always make great decisions. That's why you need a mentor. Regardless of how accomplished you are in your profession (or how many years you've been on the job), you need a mentor or coach to help you get better. Even the best athletes on the planet have coaches.

◆ *Accept a mentor* – If you are a teacher newer to the profession and your district or school assigns you a mentor – accept it. Happily. Even if you don't think you need one. Everyone, regardless of the stage of their careers, needs a mentor. If they don't assign one, seek one out. New teachers who work with a mentor report higher levels of job satisfaction and they stay in the profession longer (Harris, 2015).

◆ *Be a mentor* – If the opportunity arises, serve as a mentor (formal or informal) to someone else. The benefits go beyond just what you can offer someone. Veteran teachers who serve as a mentor for a newer colleague have higher levels of job satisfaction and most often report a renewed sense of commitment to the profession (Hammer, 2005).

◆ *Extend your reach* – If your school site seems to be short on positive role models and mentors, find supports and professional growth opportunities on the internet. Use tools like Twitter and Pinterest to find and share ideas.

◆ *Share a laugh* – Laughter is a great way to manage stress, and we are much more likely to laugh when in social situations (Provine, 2004).

◆ *Avoid negative colleagues* – Quite simply – negative colleagues suck the life out of you. In the chapter titled *Resilient Teachers Hardly Ever Spend Much Time Complaining*, I offer specific strategies for dealing with negative and burned out peers.

9

Resilient Teachers Have a Life Outside the Classroom

In a Nutshell: Striving to live a balanced life includes time spent doing things that are not related to the job. If we don't, being a teacher can consume every aspect of our life.

Digging Deeper: Educators are a dedicated and passionate group. Rightfully so – most of us view our jobs as a calling and, as a result, we give all we have in order to meet the needs of our students. For some of us, it is a fine line between being a committed and hardworking teacher and one who gets so enveloped by the profession that we neglect other important aspects of our life.

While there are lots of ways to define a "balanced life", for our purposes here, we'll address just three areas that help us to become a more resilient educator: remembering our faith tradition, attending to "ordinary things", and giving attention to passions and interests not related to the profession.

As we work to develop and refine our resilience, many of us find value, meaning, and purpose in our faith. You might be religious and you might not have a faith tradition. That's OK. The purpose here is not to proselytize or preach. Rather, it is good to remember that there is an undeniable spiritual aspect to life.

Mike Anderson, in the wonderfully practical book titled *The Well-Balanced Teacher* (2010), says that taking care of yourself includes meeting your "most basic needs". He not only includes the reminders to eat well, get adequate sleep, and exercise, he implores us to take care of our "spirit" as well. This includes engaging in spiritual growth. Plus, there is evidence that when we attend to our spiritual growth via prayer and meditation, there are physical and mental health benefits, including lower stress levels, better sleep, and a longer life (Matthews and Clark, 1999).

On top of all that, a faith provides the foundation for several elements necessary to practice resiliency such as: community and social connections, perspective when things don't make sense, a source for reframing situations, and a way to find the humor in something.

Having a life outside the classroom also means taking the time to attend to the ordinary and mundane. As hectic as life can get at times, it is important to remember to take care of the normal things in life that are not related to teaching. When we let those "normal" things pile up – when our *to-do* list is significantly longer than our *to-done* list – it adds stress to our lives.

Sometimes, the stress that we experience is self-imposed because we've let too many things pile up. If stress and control are related, a great way to manage stress is to get control over the small things. In this case, that means getting control of some things that you may have been putting off. Consider things like: balancing the checkbook, getting oil changed in the car, pulling the weeds in the backyard, going grocery shopping, or returning phone calls. When we let enough little things pile up, they become bigger stressors. So, manage your stress by dedicating time to get things done. Plus, think about how awesome you'll feel when you finally complete some of those projects that you've put off for way too long.

Even if we love our job, even if we are absolutely passionate about teaching and learning, if we become one thing, we risk burnout. As humans, we were not created as one-dimensional beings. Another way to be multi-dimensional and well-balanced is to cultivate passions and interests not related to the classroom. Consider those topics, interests, or skills that sound interesting. Everyone has a mental list (and sometimes a written list) of things we'd like to learn or do *"when we have the time"*. The truth is that you'll probably never have the amount of time you want.

So, if you've always wanted to do something like learn how to play an instrument or take a class to learn auto mechanics, do it.

I realize that the advice to spend time doing non-education related things can be difficult at times. Many of us are juggling multiple demands on our time. Maybe you're attending grad school or raising a family, or you're simply newer to the profession. I get it; this is not easy. But I also know this, resilient people take time to enjoy life away from the classroom. And, they don't feel guilty about it.

Application Points

♦ *Remember your faith tradition* – Give attention to your spiritual life and health just as you do your physical and relational health.

♦ *When home, be home* – Spend time with your family and friends. If you are like most teachers, you typically have a pile of papers to grade and an endless list of things to get done for the classroom. While those things are important, they are not as important as your family.

♦ *Cultivate a non-teaching interest* – You might just start with dreaming about those things you'd like to do and learn at some point in the future. Allow yourself to dream and then take steps, perhaps just small steps, toward those dreams.

♦ *Make a list* – Brainstorm, right now, some of those things that have been piling up and make a list. Commit to checking off two to three of those things within the next three days.

♦ *Make another list* – Sometimes called a wish list or a dream list, this one should include those things that you are interested in, passionate about, or simply want to learn more about. For example, you have likely said something like, "*When I have time, I want to learn more about…*". Dedicate time to doing those things that are interesting and enjoyable.

♦ *Calendar important items* – Many of us have great intentions but we all know where that road leads. One way to bridge the gap between intention and implementation is to dedicate specific time to doing them. When you have less-than-enjoyable tasks that need to be accomplished (like taking the dog to the vet), consider sandwiching it between two tasks that are more enjoyable. Give yourself something fun to look forward to after you've done something mundane.

♦ *Then tell people about your plans* – Most of us are more likely to follow through on a commitment if we share that commitment with someone else.

♦ *Remember the Power of "No"* – As you work to get things checked off your to-do list, consider how quickly you add more. Now might be a good time to go back and review the concepts and suggestions listed in Chapter 4.

♦ *Deal with little things when they are little* – Once you get a handle on the tasks and responsibilities you need to tackle, make a commitment going forward to not let them pile up again. For example, change the tires on your car before it's too late and you find yourself stranded on the side of the road.

10

Resilient Teachers Get Themselves Organized

In a Nutshell: Being disorganized is stressful. Manage stress by getting control of your environment, your calendar, and your responsibilities.

Digging Deeper: We've all seen them – messy desks, cluttered classrooms with piles of stuff in every corner, and learning environments so disorganized that we wonder how anything is accomplished. Common sense, along with a bit of research, tells us that environments matter. The way we organize the space, the traffic flow, the placement of visuals, the work spaces, and things like bulletin boards all matter.

But, how much does the cluttered environment matter for our success and our students' success? Fortunately, research done by Grace Chae and her colleagues offers some insights. In an interesting series of studies, they found that disorganized and cluttered environments lead to (among other things): more impulsive behavior, less focus and attention on work tasks, and less persistence at challenging tasks. They put it bluntly, "Clutter makes you a quitter" and that being in a disorganized environment depletes the mental resources necessary to be productive (Chae and Rui, 2014). While those studies were done with adults in professional work settings, the findings can offer some insights into how we organize classrooms for ourselves and our students.

Their research highlights a host of interesting questions and issues for classroom teachers. We often have to support and teach students who seem distracted, unable to focus, or who struggle to maintain persistence on a task. Could it be that a cluttered environment is making it worse for them? So, it may be time to do a room check. Put yourself in the shoes of your students (or, more accurately, put yourself in their desks) and consider the visual clutter, the organization of the learning materials, and the overall environment. While few would suggest that a sterile learning environment is best for kids, we might have to take an honest look at the clutter-factor in our classrooms. All that clutter may very well be adding to your stress and the stress of your students.

As an analogy, consider the current state of your kitchen. If you walk into your kitchen and it's messy, it smells funky, and there is no clean counter space on which to cook, you are likely to feel stressed and say something like "Oh forget it. I'll just order a pizza". However, if your kitchen is clean, smells nice, and there are only a few random utensils in the sink, you are much more likely to say, "OK, I can work with this!" The same is true of our classrooms. Just as a messy kitchen is full of distractions and stressors, so is a messy classroom.

You might say, "OK, I'm ready to de-clutter. How do I start?" Dan Triarico, in *The Zen Teacher* (2015), offers some practical suggestions: (1) **Start now and think small** – In fact, he says, "You might want to put this book down and get started right now". (2) **Ignore excuses** – The truth is that much of the clutter: the tchotchkes, the mementos, the pictures, the decorations, etc. have stories. The "story" or the background of different items may lead you to unnecessarily keep things. Sure, it would be nice if you had space for all those special rainbow pictures students have given you over the years, but we often keep things unneces-sarily. (3) **When something comes, something goes** – If you want to put up a new rainbow picture, something else will need to go. (4) **Celebrate** – When you've de-cluttered, celebrate your accom-plishment and enjoy the positive emotions that come along with tackling a long-overdue task. You might even want to celebrate with your students and ask them to keep you accountable for future de-cluttering.

When it comes to time management and organization, few people have had as big an influence as Stephen Covey. In his best seller, *The 7 Habits of Highly Effective People* (1989), he offers a concrete way to think about the different demands on our time and how we should prioritize those demands. Using a four-square matrix, consider those things in life that are urgent or not urgent and important or not important. Demands on your time range from urgent and important to not urgent and not important. Our purpose here isn't to provide a lengthy review of Covey's model; rather it is to provide a way to think about the different demands on your time. Obviously, when something is urgent and important, we devote time and attention to it and we do it well. When something is less urgent and less important, we think about it differently.

In addition to using Covey's matrix, there are other concrete steps you can take to organize and control your schedule and calendar: seek advice and suggestions from mentors and veteran teachers; block time for specific things, like grading, answering emails, returning phone calls, organizing the classroom, and personal time; use color codes to help organize different types of responsibilities; set alerts and reminders for specific tasks; and piggy-back less-than-fun tasks with something enjoyable. Finally, to help with accountability, share your calendar with students and with colleagues. You are much more likely to stay true to the schedule if you've made a commitment to someone else.

Application Points

♦ *Devote one day per week to organize* – Do this with your students. Give students time each week to clean out their desks and organize their materials. You'll be glad you did.

♦ *Return phone calls and emails in 24 hours* – The response might simply be "Thanks for the email. I will be able to follow up on _____". Don't tell people how busy you are. Everyone's busy. But an acknowledgment is helpful. If we are un-responsive to emails and phone calls, people make up stories as to why we are un-communicative (examples: we don't care, we can't manage our time well, we've given up, etc.). That's stressful for them and it is stressful for us when things pile up.

◆ *Use the "Out of Office" Assistant in email* – Most email programs allow for an automatic message to be generated when there are extended times when you won't be able to respond to messages. Often referred to as an "Out of Office" Assistant, this tool informs people that you may not be able to respond immediately.

◆ *Delegate* – In the classroom, there are many organizational tasks that students can assume. And, every classroom also has students who enjoy helping the teacher organize and take care of administrative tasks.

◆ *End the day by organizing for the next* – Before you leave at the end of the day, get all your materials, handouts, technology, and tasks ready to go for the next morning. That includes cleaning and organizing your desk and doing a quick survey of the classroom. Think about how calm and energized you'll be when you walk into your room in the morning and everything is ready to go and organized.

◆ *Arrive to meetings ten minutes early* – Showing up late to meetings is stressful. Imagine this – you are running late and you have to sneak into a meeting that has already started. What happens? All heads turn to look at you – some people give curious looks, while others roll their eyes in judgment, making you feel ashamed and small. When that happens, we sometimes feel the need to apologize or justify our tardiness. Even when we have a legitimate reason for arriving late, it's stressful. We are much better off organizing our time so that we arrive early, thus reducing stress.

◆ *Set an alarm* – In order to help you arrive early to meetings, set an alarm for 15 minutes before the meeting is scheduled to begin. In addition, set an alarm as a reminder for when it is time to go home at the end of the day.

◆ *Calendar important items* – At least once per month, spend time updating your calendar. Meet with colleagues, mentors, and family to make sure you have noted all important dates.

◆ *Calendar all important items* – Create time for family, exercise, and fun activities. Actually place those times on your calendar and promise yourself that you'll follow through on commitments. Don't feel bad or guilty carving out time for yourself. If you struggle with this, go back and re-read Chapter 1 (take care of your health) and Chapter 9 (have a life outside the classroom).

◆ *Do a room check* – If "Clutter makes you a quitter", scan your classroom from the perspective of a student and ask yourself if there are environmental factors that may make it difficult for students to be productive. Consider things like physical and visual clutter, personal space, traffic flow, and general tidiness.

◆ *Organize stuff* – Use bins, folders, file cabinets, cubbies, and other organizational tools to organize the materials and curricula in your classroom. Avoid the temptation to pile things up in a corner. For organization tips and suggestions, seek advice from a mentor or veteran teacher (and of course steal good ideas from the internet).

◆ *Make a to-do list* – In the previous chapter, we explored the power of lists to organize and prioritize our lives. The same strategies work here – make a list of those important tasks and responsibilities, and devote time on a daily basis to update your lists.

11

Resilient Teachers Focus on What They Can Control

In a Nutshell: It's not much more complicated than this: a constant focus on what is beyond your control will make you miserable. You don't want to be the source of your own misery and stress. We are much better off when we focus on what is within our control and influence.

Digging Deeper: In his book *Man's Search for Meaning*, Holocaust survivor Viktor Frankl famously said *"Everything can be taken from a man but one thing: the last of the human freedoms – to choose one's attitude in any given set of circumstances, to choose one's own way"* (Frankl, 1984). What we choose to focus on – those things that we let occupy our minds – has a significant influence on our ability to manage stress and practice resilience.

Since the definition of stress is a perception of a lack of control, it makes sense that focusing on what we *can* control is a great way to combat stress. And, recall that we've narrowed resilience down to two simple things: our mindsets and our coping mechanisms – *how we think* about the challenges in front of us and *what we do* when the times get tough. When we focus on what we can control and where we have influence, we actually do a little of each of those.

Application Points

We probably don't need a 2,000 word chapter to tell us what you already know. So, we'll keep it brief and do two simple but powerful exercises.

◆ *Exercise #1 – Create a T-Chart* – Label the left-hand column "Control" and the right-hand column "Cannot Control". Take a few moments and brainstorm those things, within the classroom and school environment, that are within your control and those that are not. Consider both big and small, ordinary and unusual, and daily routines. To get started, consider things like:

   ◆ Your class schedule
   ◆ The number of students you serve who have Individualized Education Plans (IEPs)
   ◆ Lesson design and delivery
   ◆ Standardized assessments
   ◆ Who will complete your annual evaluation
   ◆ How students are greeted to begin each day
   ◆ Coaching or extra-curricular assignments
   ◆ Which committees you'll serve on
   ◆ How your classroom is organized
   ◆ Who you eat lunch with
   ◆ How often and how parents are contacted
   ◆ How you celebrate student successes
   ◆ Who you collaborate with

That's not an exhaustive list, of course. But the big idea is that there are things that are within our control and there are things that are not. This is true of every job in every industry. The more we focus our time and effort on those areas where we have control, the less stressed we'll be.

◆ *Exercise #2 – Imagine this scenario* – It's the end of a long school day and an irritated parent enters your classroom and confronts you about what they believe to be inequitable grading practices. They make claims that are untrue, they exaggerate, and they threaten. They do this while in the presence of their child. This puts you on the defensive and you feel your stress levels rapidly increase. In this situation, there are several things that you cannot control: the other person's emotions, the accuracy of their beliefs, the audience, or the timing of the interaction. But what do you have control over? Obviously, first and foremost you have control over how you respond. You can control: your tone of voice, the questions you ask, your non-verbals, and your thinking patterns and assumptions about the other person's motives. By the way, one of the reasons that other people (such as the parent in this example) sometimes behave the way they do is because they are attempting to take control because they feel stressed about the confrontation. When interacting with people who are being less than productive and helpful, it is good to remember that they are often experiencing increased stress levels and they are attempting to take control in order to manage that stress.

12

Resilient Teachers Know How to Receive Feedback

In a Nutshell: As educators, feedback is all around us. Whether it comes from external sources (students, colleagues, parents, formal evaluations, etc.) or from our own personal reflections, there is no shortage of information at our disposal. However, what matters as much as the source of the feedback is the mindset we put ourselves into in order to receive (and ultimately act upon) that feedback.

Digging Deeper: For our purposes here, we'll adopt Grant Wiggins's definition of feedback – actionable or useful information about how we are doing in our efforts to reach a goal (Wiggins, 2012). More specifically, feedback is information about *the gap* between our performance and that desired goal (Wiliam, 2016).

Related to life in the classroom, there are two key concepts to consider. First, true feedback is simply information. Not to be confused with praise, advice, or criticism, feedback is information in the form of data, facts, or descriptions that we can act upon in order to improve our practice. The second important thing to consider is the fact that true feedback is actionable; that is, we must be able to do something with the information that we receive. We might receive useful and helpful information, but if no action is taken, it cannot be considered feedback.

Let's take that idea (that feedback must be acted upon) one level deeper. Imagine that you give your students a test and half of them fail it. In this case, grades are information – both for us and for our students. If, after looking at the grades, we say something like "Oh well, we'll try to do better next time. We've got another unit to cover", then, regardless of how accurate, timely, or important the information is, it won't become feedback until we do something with it.

This idea that feedback is actionable information is essential to our understanding of how to build, practice, and refine our resilience. If part of being resilient is figuring out how to take control of different aspects of our life, knowing how to receive feedback is important. We receive tons of information on a daily basis in the form of data, descriptions, narratives, facts, student grades, complaints, compliments, memos, meeting notes, administrative directives, etc. But it is only that information that we act upon that can make much of a difference. Knowing both how to receive and act upon all this information is core to being resilient.

Feedback is essential. Not too many well-informed educators will argue that fact. It is essential for our students, it is essential for our own personal growth, and it is foundational to the ability to become more resilient. But there is one thing that is often overlooked when it comes to feedback – *how do we receive it?* Having actionable information at our disposal is pointless unless we have the mindset and tools to grapple with it. So, here are four ideas that will help make feedback useful:

1. **Acknowledge that receiving feedback can be emotional**. Those emotions might range from pride to disappointment, from confusion to outright rejection. When we have to deal with information about our status or growth, it can elicit a range of emotions that must be dealt with. It's OK to have an emotional reaction to feedback, particularly when that information/feedback conflicts with your own beliefs or opinions. Think about this way – if we put forth a decent amount of effort toward mastering a skill or completing a task and then we don't quite meet expectations, it can be devastating. In essence, it's normal to be disappointed when you fail to meet either your own expectations or the expectations of others. It's also

normal to feel pride and relief when you do well. And, recall what we discussed in Chapter 5 – we cannot control our emotions, but we can manage them.

2. **Understand that feedback is about the task or progress, not the person.** The more we work to separate the information from the person, the better off we'll be. Feedback is about my progress and my growth, it's not about my worth, value, or identity. This is a fine line of course and it's easy to understand from a purely logical point of view. It's much more difficult, of course, to put into practice when you are on the receiving end of feedback that might elicit an emotional response. But the more we remind ourselves that feedback is less about the person and more about growth, the more likely we'll employ the effort to act on the feedback.

3. **Concede that feedback is often subjective**. As much as the feedback might come in the form of evaluations, scales, checklists, or models, feedback is typically subjective in nature. When feedback is subjective, mistakes can be made and situations misunderstood. This is an essential characteristic of feedback – the information we receive has been filtered through someone else's perspective. We understand this not to be dismissive of the opinions of others but to understand it. Even when the feedback comes from a credible and reliable source, it has typically been filtered or edited according to the opinions, beliefs, or perspectives of the person providing the feedback.

4. **Ask questions about the feedback.** When faced with information that might conflict with your own beliefs or opinions, take the time to reflect and ask questions. Remind yourself that the information is not personal, it's about progress. If needed, review the feedback with a mentor or a trusted colleague. Most specifically, ask yourself, "How can I use this information to improve?" When we adopt this mindset, it not only helps us to consider where we can take action but also supports our resilience by helping to clarify where we have control.

Application Points

♦ *Understand the difference between feedback and evaluation* – While these two terms are often used synonymously in education, they are very different. They serve two different purposes that, while they may be complimentary, are not the same. Evaluation results in judgments, statements of value, or determinations. Feedback is simply the information about progress or status. Evaluations are typically formal; feedback can be formal or informal.

♦ *Seek feedback* – In their article *Find the Coaching in Criticism*, authors Sheila Heen and Douglas Stone, highlight the fact that seeking feedback by asking for specific information helps you not only to improve your practice but also helps to shape how the other person views you. They say, "… when you ask for feedback, you not only find out how others see you, you also *influence* how they see you. Soliciting constructive criticism communicates humility, respect, passion for excellence, and confidence, all in one go".

♦ *Design your own feedback methods* – Feedback does not always have to come from an external source, and it does not necessarily need to be prompted by someone else. Gather your own data and information, reflect upon it, and take action. Manage feedback-related stress by taking control and taking action. A great way to do this is by audio recording a lesson. Listen to yourself as you teach, guide, and direct students.

♦ *Acknowledge that there is much you don't know* – Regardless of the number of years of experience under your belt, you still have a lot to learn.

♦ *Don't expect perfect ratings* – When it comes to formal evaluations or informal classroom walkthroughs done by leadership, don't always expect that you'll receive perfect ratings or feedback, even if you've gotten them in the past. Consider that if you do get perfect ratings year after year, you are probably not trying anything new or taking any risks in the classroom. Consider also how we respond when a student questions a less-than-perfect score on an assignment, "Why didn't I get 100"? Don't we often tell them something like, "No one is perfect. It's OK. You still got a great score"?

◆ *Admit your faults* – There are great teachers, not perfect ones. And, as we strive to get better and improve we'll make mistakes. Author Sir Ken Robinson said it well: "If you're not prepared to be wrong, you'll never come up with anything original".

◆ *Quit taking it personally (QTIP)* – As much as possible, adopt the QTIP mindset. When you are truly open to receiving feedback, there will undoubtedly be times when you don't like the feedback you get. Do your best to not take the criticism personally. It's a fine line, of course. You don't want to go through life being cold-hearted and pretending that nothing gets to you but you also don't want to be so sensitive that you find offense when none was intended.

◆ *Advocate* – If something seems amiss or inaccurate regarding the feedback you are receiving, take control and action by advocating for yourself. Seek clarification, ask questions, and dig for insights. We'll talk more about how to advocate for yourself in the next chapter.

◆ *Consider triggers* – Feedback often triggers strong emotions. If you find yourself experiencing frustration, confusion, irritation, or anger, remember that emotions cannot be controlled but they can be managed. When you find yourself experiencing those strong emotions, go back and review the suggestions for Triggers (Chapter 6) and In-the-Moment Stress Relievers (Chapter 7).

◆ *Bonus idea* – Model the use of actionable information and feedback for your students. Don't just expect that students respond appropriately to feedback; show them how to do it.

13

Resilient Teachers Advocate for Themselves

In a Nutshell: To advocate for yourself – to take specific action to meet your own needs – is an essential resiliency tool. Rather than viewing themselves as victims or powerless during challenging times, resilient teachers recognize where they have influence and take specific steps to get their needs met.

Digging Deeper: An advocate (the noun version of the word) is a person who speaks up, provides support, or intervenes on behalf of another. More specifically, an advocate is one who *publicly* supports a cause, an issue, or an individual. An advocate is one who can assess a situation and determine what issues need to be addressed and where changes should take place. In the legal world, there are court-appointed special advocates (CASAs) whose job it is to speak up on behalf of those who are unable to do so for themselves.

To advocate (as a verb) is to take action to bridge the gap between what should be and what is. When we advocate for something, we seek to help, intercede, or take action in order to improve conditions or make things right. While many of us are quick to advocate for someone else (our students, for example), some of us are a bit slower to speak up on our own behalf. When you see something amiss in your school or organization – something that is negatively impacting your ability to do your job effectively – take control by being your own champion. After all, we encourage our students to advocate for themselves, we should do the same.

Concepts related to self-advocacy are rooted in research on self-efficacy. Popularized by world-renowned psychologist Albert Bandura in the 1980s, in essence self-efficacy is the belief that what you do matters; what specific steps you take in life help to determine outcomes and experiences. He defines it this way, "*Self-efficacy is the belief in one's ability to influence events that effect one's life and control over the way these events are experienced* (Bandura, 1997)". And, he goes on to make connections between self-efficacy and control, "*If people believe they have no power to produce results, they will not attempt to make things happen*".

Individuals with higher levels of belief in their ability to influence outcomes (which is what we call self-efficacy) are more resilient and have lower levels of anxiety (Saks, 1994; Li and Nishikawa, 2012). From a broad perspective, we can think of this way – part of being resilient consists of our thinking patterns. Self-efficacy is that internal belief that we can influence what happens to us. It is first and foremost a belief system. In recent years, Dr. Carol Dweck has made the connection between mindsets and external behavior as eloquently and convincingly as anyone. Our beliefs and internal dialogues influence behavior. Self-advocacy also supports the second part of being resilient: the coping mechanisms we use to manage stress.

Application Points

- *Don't wait until you're stressed* – Be proactive about taking care of your own needs. As previously discussed, this relates to our physical health (Chapter 1) but also relates to addressing those things in your work or school environment that could be improved. Resilient teachers also know themselves well enough to anticipate their needs.
- *Get help* – There will be times when you need assistance, guidance, and direction. Advocate for yourself by getting help and seeking the advice, wisdom, and insights of mentors and trusted colleagues.

◆ *Get the facts* – When advocating for yourself, make sure that you are doing so with all the facts. While feelings, emotions, and personal beliefs are important, the essence of advocation is to try to influence another's point of view or to prompt them to take action. We are best served by asserting our influence based on facts along with emotions and personal beliefs.

◆ *Plan your efforts* – When it comes to advocating for yourself, plan it out. While there certainly will be times when you need to speak up and advocate on a moment's notice, you'll be best served with a thoughtful, planned approach.

◆ *Ask for clarification* – During conversations focused on change, seek clarification from others. Don't assume that you've communicated clearly enough that everyone understands your perspectives or beliefs. Ask follow up questions and maintain a stance of humility and openness.

◆ *Offer solutions* – Part of advocating is seeking a change. Part of seeking a change is having an idea of not only what needs to change but how to change it. As you plan to speak up for yourself, be ready to answer the question, *"What should we do next?"* In other words, advocating for something is twofold – seeing what needs to change and having an idea of how to change it.

◆ *But, I don't have any solutions* – There will be times when you have a clear idea of what needs to change, but you genuinely don't know how to change it. In those cases, don't shy away from speaking up. There may be times when you'll simply need to say, *"I know this needs to change but I'm not sure how to get it done"*. In those cases, acknowledge this fact and ask to work together to find solutions.

◆ *Recognize emotions* – During times of stress or conflict, powerful emotions often arise. As you speak up for yourself, recognize and acknowledge that emotions may be influencing your perspective.

◆ *Maintain realistic expectations* – Don't always expect immediate results. We work in systems and organizations. There are procedures, structures, and a hierarchy that must be dealt with. Even when a path to improvement is clear and agreed upon, it can take time to see results.

◆ *Take a seat on the balcony* – When we are advocating for a change or seeking to influence an outcome, it is helpful to keep a couple of things in mind. First, yours is only one perspective. It very well might be the "right" one but it is good to remember that you are rarely as right as you think you are and the other person is rarely 100% wrong. Second, current beliefs are always influenced by past events or circumstances. Ask yourself if you are holding on to an idea or belief primarily because of past hurts or offenses. Step back and attempt to view the situation as an outsider might: sitting on the balcony watching it all play out.

◆ *Remember, you are not a victim* – While you may have been *victimized* by a person or a situation, it is your belief that either holds you back or moves you forward. Life is 10% what happens to you and 90% how you respond. That percentage breakdown has been attributed to Chuck Swindoll, the Texas-based minister who is famous for his Insight for Living radio program. While it makes for a great slogan, it is also a powerful mindset. In his book *The Happiness Equation* (2016), Neil Pasricha puts it this way – that 90% is made up of how we view the world; how we perceive the things happening around us. He goes on to say that the 90% is made up largely by intentional actions. For our discussion here, those intentional actions include self-advocating when things need to change.

14

Resilient Teachers Create and Track Goals

In a Nutshell: If being resilient is all about recognizing and gaining control, what better way to manage the stressors of the unknown than to create and track goals. Goals are empowering, even if we don't always reach them.

Digging Deeper: We'll start this chapter with something different. Below I've listed several quotes* – some famous, some not as well known – that will get us to think about the nature, power, and influence of goals. Read, reflect, and select one or two that are meaningful to you.

> Leonardo Da Vinci woke up in the morning and made a list of what he wanted to learn. I wake up and check the news on my phone
>
> –Austin Kleon (2019)

> If you don't fill up your day with challenges that inspire you, your day will be filled up with challenges that don't inspire you
>
> –Unknown

> The best time to plant a tree was 20 years ago. The second best time is now.
>
> –Chinese Proverb

> Yes, there is a danger in setting goals but the risk is infin-
> itely greater when you don't set goals.
>
> –Zig Ziglar (1977)

> The thing about goals is that living without them is a lot
> more fun, in the short run. It seems to me, though, that
> the people who get things done, who lead, who grow and
> who make an impact… those people have goals.
>
> –Seth Godin (2009)

> If you are not failing often, clearly your goals are set too
> low. Every great person's life has failures but they were
> defined by their successes.
>
> –Dr. Eric Jensen

Goals. That very word strikes fear into many people. Why is that? Why do we sometimes find ourselves shying away from creating and tracking goals? It may be due to a fear of failure or we may be simply too busy to take the time to create them. Regardless of where you are on the love-hate continuum with goals, there is an essential connection to resiliency that is important to understand. Namely, when we take the time to create, track, and reflect upon self-directed goals, it is empowering.

There are countless experts who have written about the power of goals. There is no shortage of opinion, beliefs, research, and suggestions about the best place to start. Should we write SMART goals (specific, measurable, attainable, realistic, timely) or should our goals be HARD (heart-felt, animated, required difficult)? As teachers, should we adopt the goals of the overall school or should we create personal ones? What about the best form of accountability?

The questions and variables are vast. Our purpose here is not to review the pros and cons of different models but rather to make one very specific and powerful connection – goals allow a sense of control and influence during a time when stress is typically high. As teachers, we are constantly under the expectation that we improve our practice and get better at our jobs. Rightfully so, by the way; there should be an expectation that we improve because our effectiveness impacts children and families. Resilient teachers realize this essential connection and take specific steps (via creating and tracking goals) in order to manage stress and improve their craft. Resilient teachers take control and influence the process of creating and tracking goals; they don't act as passive recipients of someone else's goal-setting process.

While we won't do an overview of the literature on goals, we will highlight two important topics as they relate to goals as a way to practice resiliency. Specifically, we'll look at the concept of being future-minded and we'll consider how best to respond when we face setbacks or failure.

Being future-minded simply means to think about the future in a positive light (Allen, 2019). Sometimes referred to as "prospection", it is a thinking pattern that helps us to consider alternative outcomes for the future. Specifically, being future-minded focuses on positive outcomes based on factors that are under our control. Often studied under the broad category of a psychological concept called *agency*, it is the idea that we can cause desirable things to happen to us (Osman, 2014). It is a thinking pattern and a decision-making process in the brain that supports the achievement of concrete goals (Medea et al., 2018). The main message is this – how we think about the future matters in terms of our stress management and resiliency. One practical thing we can do to be future-minded is to create and track goals.

The process of creating and tracking goals, assuming you are taking sufficient risks and pushing yourself outside your comfort zone, will result in setbacks and failure. There will simply be times when you strike out. Side note, if you always reach your goals – if you hit a home run every time you come up to bat – you are not stretching yourself enough. You might be capable of playing in the big leagues but if you quarantine yourself to the minor leagues because of a fear of failure, you'll never know how great you can be. Don't let a fear of failure hold you back.

With that pep-talk floating around in your mind, it is good to have some concrete steps to take when you fail to reach a goal. First, it's OK to be disappointed or frustrated. It's normal to feel let down when you've put effort into something. So, give yourself permission to experience the emotion, but don't wallow; feel, process, reflect, and move on. Second, remind yourself that failure is normal. We expect our kids to try hard enough that they will occasionally miss the mark. We need to adopt that same mentality for ourselves. Next, as you reflect on what you've learned through the process, remember what leadership guru John Maxwell advises: you can either fail backward or you can fail forward. Failing forward is a proactive mental stance where we look for the positive benefits that might come from a negative experience (Maxwell, 2007). Finally, don't beat yourself up for failing to meet the goal. We'll talk more about this in the chapter titled "Resilient Teachers Hardly Ever Beat Themselves Up Over Past Mistakes".

Application Points

- *Collaborate* – The process of creating, tracking, achieving (or not achieving) goals should be a team sport. Seek the help from mentors, colleagues, coaches, administrators, and even students. If you work in a school or a system where you are required to write and track annual goals, work together with a team of like-minded professionals who can support your journey.
- *Get a coach* – When we are coached toward a goal, we are more likely to reach that goal, and we are more likely to increase our resiliency and manage work-place stress (Grant et al., 2009). If an academic coach is available, seek their support. If one is not available, find one. Coaches are essential because it is very difficult to get better just on our own.
- *Be specific* – Almost every format, template, or model for creating goals calls for specificity. There is a good reason for this. Aside from the obvious (you can't reach a goal if you have no target), it turns out that the brain loves specificity, particularly in relation to setting goals. The brain seems to be hard-wired to accomplish goals and when we have a clear goal in front of us, the brain rallies the necessary cognitive and executive functions needed to tackle the goal (Miller and Cohen, 2001).

- *Celebrate* – Yup, that's it – just a reminder to celebrate when you achieve something good.
- *Beware of hypocrisy* – Every day we challenge our students to learn more, improve, be better, experience new things, and to take risks. If we are not willing to do the same, we risk being a hypocrite and losing credibility.
- *Harness the power of deadlines* – Resilient teachers harness the power of deadlines to help reach goals. The truth is that deadlines and accountability are your best friends when attempting to reach a goal.
- *Enlist a friend* – Mentors, friends, and trusted colleagues not only help with the creation of goals, they can help with accountability as well. Consider Jenny Craig's secret sauce – what makes her model of weight loss so successful? It's not the food. It's the fact that there are high levels of accountability. When we are accountable for our goals, we are more likely to take the steps necessary to reach them.
- *Prepare for setbacks* – If we truly create challenging goals, there will be times when we stumble. Dr. Peter Gollwitzer, a researcher who has spent much of his career studying goals, advises the use of "implementation intentions" as way to pre-plan a response to a setback. Typically phrased as an "If-then" response, the idea is to think ahead and plan a response to an obstacle. We are more likely to be successful if we do two things: realize that setbacks are likely and plan a specific response when faced with that setback.
- *Use web-based tools* – Two of my favorites are www. futureme.org and www.goalscape.com. Future me allows you to write an email that will be sent to yourself at a self-determined time in the future. It serves as a sort of letter from your future self. Goalscape.com offers many of the same features as other online resources but uses visual tools to track and prioritize goals.

*As with the nature of quotes, it is sometimes difficult to track down the original source or context of the quote, so all the above should rather say "attributed to".

15

Resilient Teachers Unplug

In a Nutshell: The sheer amount of information coming at us on a daily basis is staggering – emails, texts, radio, TV, gaming, etc. It can be overwhelming. Resilient teachers take regular opportunities to de-stress by taking a break from the onslaught of digital data.

Digging Deeper: As mentioned in the chapter on the power of saying no, some of us struggle with FOMO – *the fear of missing out.* We want to keep up with the latest Facebook posts from our friends and family, we enjoy the popular memes floating around on Snapchat and Twitter, and we want to stay current on the news and current issues that impact our profession. While it certainly is important to stay connected and tuned in, there are simply times when we need to let it all go.

Some people refer to this concept as a "digital diet" or "digital detox". The idea is that there is power (and control) in simply stepping away from the devices for a period of time. When we take time to unplug, even for a few minutes, we allow our brains to recalibrate and take a break from the sheer quantity of information attacking us at any given time. This often brings a sense of calm, a renewed sense of your own priorities, and some confidence that you can indeed survive without being tethered to a device.

Some of us rely on our devices to help us multi-task. But the truth is you can't; there is no such thing as multi-tasking. It's a myth. Far too many of us have fallen victim to the appealing idea that we can accomplish multiple things at the same time. But you cannot. Without going into great lengths about the role of attention and the brain, suffice it to say that you can only pay attention to one thing at a time. More specifically, you can only *consciously* process and focus on one thing at a time. Here is the real definition of multi-tasking: screwing up several things simultaneously.

When we attempt to multi-task, what our brains are actually doing is task-switching. Since our brains can only consciously process one thing at a time, when we attempt to multi-task, what our brain actually does is switch between tasks or areas of focus. Some of us can do this task-switching very rapidly. So, you might say, "That sounds fine to me, what's the problem?" While some of us are adept at task-switching rapidly, there is always a cognitive loss or a "switch cost" as some researchers refer to it (Altman, 2017). All this means is that when we attempt to use our devices to accomplish multiple things at the same time, it impacts our ability to do any of those things well.

Imagine this: you are grading papers while at the same time preparing dinner for your family. You might think you are multi-tasking when in reality you are switching (perhaps quickly) between two different things that require your attention. For example, you are in the middle of grading a paper when a timer goes off. You stop grading the paper and take the meal out of the oven. Since your attention has been split (albeit for a short period of time), when you go back to grading the paper, you will need to take a moment to remember where you left off. In essence, there is a loss of "flow" and an impact on short-term memory. When we do this often, the brain becomes fatigued and we make more mistakes. Bottom-line, you are better off focusing on just one thing at a time. For efficiency and accuracy, set aside the devices because they'll end up splitting your attention. For a deeper dive into this phenomenon, read John Medina's book *Brain Rules* (2008). In that book, he devotes an entire chapter to the role of attention in the brain, and he addresses the damage done when we attempt to multi-task.

All that time on a device comes at a price; this "hyper-connectivity" can be a double-edged sword. The good news about devices such as smartphones is that they allow us to stay connected. The bad news is that not all those connections are healthy, beneficial, or supportive of our resilience. If we are honest with ourselves, many of us would admit that the constant flow of information and connection is increasing our stress, not reducing it.

Tonya Goodwin, in the book *Off: Your Digital Detox to a Better Life*, reminds us that devices such as smartphones are neither good or bad, they are simply tools. Like with any tool, it all comes down to how it is used. Some of us, if we are honest, are addicted. We'd have trouble attending a staff meeting without checking our phones five to six times every hour. Goodwin advises, "Regaining balance from any addiction starts with setting boundaries. It's not that we are using screens at all that's the problem, it's that we are using them without limits". So, set yourself some limits. In the end, although it might be difficult to step away, you'll find those limits are empowering.

Application Points

- ◆ *Consider the hold that your electronics may have on you.* Simply ask yourself, does this device connect me to the important things in my life or does it isolate me from them? Do I use this tool to enhance my work or do I use it to avoid it? Does the device bring me closer to those people I value or do I use it as an excuse to avoid them?
- ◆ *Find the power button and turn it off.* Yes, actually find the power switch and power down. At the very least, turn off your alerts. Remember life before smartphones? Somehow we managed to get along just fine.
- ◆ *Analyze your usage.* If you've not done this before, it takes some guts. Try one of the web-based apps or programs that provide data on the amount of time you spend on your device.
- ◆ *If you are having trouble sleeping, stop the use of all electronic devices for an hour before you want to fall asleep.* The blue light emitted from devices such as smartphones and tablets suppress melatonin, which impacts the ability to fall asleep (University of Haifa, 2017).

◆ *Resist the temptation to multi-task*. You'll get things done faster and make fewer mistakes if you simply focus on one thing at a time.

◆ *If you are not ready to go cold-turkey, start small*. Go for a 15 minute-walk without your phone, have a five-minute conversation without checking email, or leave the devices in your car when you go out for a meal.

◆ *Use your device-free time to catch up on important things*. There are no doubt things that you want or need to do and a constant focus on a device is preventing you from doing them. So, read a book, write a letter, exercise, play a board game, talk to your family, clean out the garage, take the dog for a walk, bring the neighbor some cookies, etc.

16

Resilient Teachers Laugh and Have Fun with Their Students

In a Nutshell: Being a teacher is serious business. A lot rides on how effective we are at our jobs. While we should treat our duties with the thoughtful attention they deserve, we do well to remember that fun really matters. Laughter, play, and joy (and even silliness at times) go a long way in helping to manage stress.

Digging Deeper: Before we take a look at why this topic matters so much, quick question – when was the last time you had fun with your students? When was the last time you laughed, acted a bit silly, or did something truly enjoyable with them? Hopefully, the answer is *not too long ago*.

To start off, I realize that not everything can be fun in school. Classrooms are places with often competing priorities – testing, schedules, curricular demands, and the like are not always within the direct control of classroom teachers. I get that.

While not everything can be fun, it's important to know that when classroom activities are fun, enjoyable, and pleasurable, some amazing things happen. Most notably, when activities are perceived as fun, the brain responds with a release of the neurotransmitter dopamine. This is true for both teachers and students. Fun activities make teaching and learning well, fun. Why does dopamine matter? It's the chemical most commonly associated with pleasure and reward. When we experience something enjoyable, our brains reward us with good feelings as if to say, "Hey, that felt good. Remember to do that again". Not only does dopamine make us feel good, it helps with attention, motivation, and memory. Bottom-line – dopamine is a classroom teacher's best friend.

The evidence supporting the importance of fun, humor, and laughter in relation to managing stress is emerging but convincing. Consider just some of what we know:

- ◆ Lee Berk from Loma Linda University has been described as the world's leading authority on laughter. Among other health benefits, he notes that anticipating a laugh reduces stress (Berk, 2006).
- ◆ Smiling releases serotonin and dopamine, both of which help to regulate mood and make you feel better.
- ◆ Teacher stress is contagious. One study found that when elementary teachers had elevated cortisol levels, so did their students (Oberle and Schonert-Reichl, 2016).
- ◆ As previously stated, happiness isn't necessarily our goal; happiness is a byproduct of other things going on in our lives. But one thing that makes most people happy is doing something fun. And, happier people tend to have better overall health and lower stress levels (Steptoe et al., 2008).
- ◆ Merely labeling something as "fun" helps our most underachieving students the most (Hart and Albarracín, 2009).
- ◆ Mike Anderson, in *The Well-Balanced Teacher* (2010), reminds us that we are better people when we laugh and have fun. He notes, "When we are having fun, we can also let small annoyances roll off our backs more easily, and we have more positive energy for our students."
- ◆ Human babies learn to laugh before they learn to speak.

Regardless of the weight of the evidence, if you're not having fun in your job you likely dread going to work each day. In fact, teaching probably then becomes a four-letter word – *work*. Don't get me wrong – I know that teaching is hard work. It can be exhausting at times. But the main message is this – having fun can help buffer the stressors that come along with classroom teaching.

If part of you says something like *"We don't have time for 'fun'. We've got too many standards to teach and too many important assessments to master"*, I sympathize. You're right. You have way too much to do and getting students to master standards and do well on assessments *is* important. But what if having fun in the learning environment led to greater levels of academic achievement for your students? In fact, studies have found just that – when learning is infused with fun, wonder, and laugher, students retain more content knowledge (Banas et al., 2011). Learning is serious, but it doesn't have to be boring and tedious.

It's important to make a distinction between humor and sarcasm. For most of my career as an educational leader, speaker, and author, I have warned educators about the negative effects of using sarcasm in the classroom. The "lowest form of wit", as Oscar Wilde famously said, often finds itself sneaking its way into our classrooms.

I came across a blog by a high school math teacher by the name of Robert Ahdoot who explained the negative effects of sarcasm as eloquently as I've ever read. In fact, he said it so well, it bears repeating here.

> We need to understand that the core act of learning is really an act of vulnerability. Students expose themselves to potential embarrassment, shame and failure when venturing into the waters of what they don't know. And they need to learn the stuff you're offering, under a time crunch, through fatigue, stress and pressure. Within this framework, present yourself as their ally. Allies, by nature, must make the lives of their partners easier. Forcing students to decode what you may mean — especially if they're already baffled — inevitably makes their lives harder.
>
> (Ahdoot, 2016)

Quite simply, sarcasm sets students up for, at best, confusion and internal turmoil. At worst, we are creating enemies. From the perspective of the brain, think about the emotional responses we invoke when we make students the brunt of a sarcastic comment. Harvard professor Francesca Gino (2015) said it well, "As a form of communication, sarcasm takes on the debt of conflict." Humor is extremely powerful and can do wonders in the classroom as a learning and relationship tool. Let's just not confuse sarcasm with humor.

Application Points

◆ *Find small ways* – During a typical school year, there are times when the stressors seem to magnify – parent conferences, standardized testing, formal evaluations, etc. It is during those times when finding ways, even small ways, to have fun is especially important.

◆ *Share a laugh* – Sharing a laugh is a great way of connecting and strengthening relationships with students, families, colleagues, and administrators. Demonstrating a sense of humor – particularly when you are able to laugh at yourself – shows a high level of maturity.

◆ *Avoid sarcasm* – Resilient teachers have a sense of humor but never at the expense of kids, our colleagues, parents, administration, or the larger educational community.

◆ *Schedule time for fun* – Allen Mendler – author of *The Resilient Teacher* (2014) suggests that for teaching to be satisfying that it needs to be fun or "playful" 25% of the time. Now, that may be a challenge depending on the school culture or environment you work in. But think about the intersection between what you enjoy and what your students enjoy.

◆ *Enlist the help of the class clown* – Allow them to tell knock-knock jokes, tell funny stories, or lighten the mood after serious learning.

◆ *Ask students* – Do some informal surveying of your students with questions like, "What was the most fun thing we did this year?" and "What changes could I make next year in order to make the lessons more fun and engaging?"

◆ *Don't be afraid to be silly* – Wear the goofy hats, sit on the floor and play games, listen to knock-knock jokes, dance, bring out the Mad Libs, and tell silly stories. You might say, "But, I'm just not a silly person. It's not my personality". I get that. We are all wired differently. Don't think that you have to become a different person, merely let yourself let loose enough to have some fun because you'll feel better and so will your students.

17

Resilient Teachers Help Students Build Resiliency

In a Nutshell: If teachers are able to manage stress better by practicing resilience, what better gift could we offer our students than to help them do the same?

Digging Deeper: Before we dig into application points and specific strategies, it is important to remember that resiliency (and stress management in general) can only be developed by the individual. We cannot develop resiliency in anyone else. It has to be personally refined and practiced. Much like learning to read has to take place within the mind of the individual, learning to be resilient is a personal process that involves an interplay between our backgrounds, beliefs, opinions, and experiences. Like learning to read, there are some good practices and general guidelines that are effective under most circumstances, but every child and every situation is unique. Ultimately, each individual needs to grapple with the concepts and put the skills into practice in their own lives.

So, what can we do? We can place students in situations, contexts, and conditions where they think about, learn, and refine their own understanding of resiliency. More importantly, we can do this often in a preventative, low-stakes environment. The analogy of learning to read works here as well. If we want a child to learn to read, we offer them lots of support, encouragement, enjoyment, varied experiences, differentiated learning opportunities, and feedback as a preventative, forward-thinking, and planned process. We don't wait until it is too late to teach a child to read; we don't wait until they need to start reading before we teach them to read. This may be a nuanced point, but it is an important one: we teach kids how to read *before* they need to know how to read. And, we don't wait until the stakes are too high (a standardized test, for example) before we give them the knowledge, skills, and background experiences they need. It is the same for helping students build resiliency and stress management. We know that students will need these skills. Let's not wait until they are in the midst of a crisis to help them develop them.

If you are looking for a school-wide resource or something curriculum-based, here are some great places to start:

- ◆ *Fostering Resilient Learners* by Kristin Souers with Pete Hall
- ◆ *Building Resilient Students* by Kate Thomsen
- ◆ *All Learning is Social and Emotional* by Nancy Frey, Doug Fisher, and Dominique Smith
- ◆ *Trauma-Sensitive Schools* by Susan Craig
- ◆ *MindUp* curriculum developed by the Goldie Hawn Foundation

Some of our students experience tremendous stressors in their daily lives. Some have been victimized or abused, some live in dysfunctional homes, and some are dealing with the negative effects of poverty. We already know what unchecked stress does to our brains and bodies (hint: it's not good), but a quick review here is helpful. Stress is the body's response to a perception of a lack of control. Many of our students come from homes that seem out of control, chaotic, or unhealthy. When the brain senses that it needs to gain control, it releases a host of chemicals (primarily cortisol and adrenaline) that have one primary purpose: to get control. Cortisol and adrenaline are designed to provide the necessary physical and cognitive resources necessary to gain back some control. Not all stress is unhealthy, mind you. But when stress is long-term, unchecked, and we don't have a good way to deal with it, it becomes toxic and dangerous.

Specific application points are described below, but almost any of the strategies and ideas we've discussed in the previous chapters will work well for our students. For example, students should be given the opportunity to express gratitude, shown how to reframe situations, reminded to the power of emotions, and taught to advocate for themselves. Now might be a good time to review the previous chapters and make some notes about how those practices and ideas could be used with students.

Application Points

- *Prioritize relationships* – Before we attempt to help students develop resiliency, remember that everything revolves around trusting relationships. Everything. All our efforts will fall short unless students trust us and feel safe in our presence.
- *Teach about conflict* – Preview the ideas in the chapter titled *Resilient Teachers Hardly Ever Shy Away from Conflict* and isolate concepts and strategies that your children can understand.
- *Teach how to offer and accept an apology* – Speaking of conflict, there are times when students need to apologize to each other. And, there are times when students need to accept an apology offered to them. Teach them specific phrases, body posture, and thinking patterns that support the delivery and acceptance of an apology.
- *Institute daily quiet time* – Dr. William Bender, author of the book *20 Disciplinary Strategies for Working with Challenging Students* (2015), describes a simple but powerful method to help students gain control over various aspects of their lives, including mood, breathing, and general attitude toward school. By simply providing time each day for students to practice being still and silent, students gain an understanding of what they can control and how they can influence their own thinking. Dr. Bender suggests a significant reduction in misbehavior and an increase in school attendance when a short, daily quiet time is instituted.

◆ *Provide concrete examples* – Don't just tell kids about resiliency, don't just define it, show them real examples of things that are resilient. Any of the following could be used as an object lesson to describe the nature and characteristics of something that is resilient: rubber bands, glow sticks (they have to be broken or cracked before they shine), a pencil and an eraser, a raw spaghetti noodle, a balloon, or War Heads candy (they start out sour, then turn sweet).

◆ *Share stories of success* – Share stories of how people have practiced resiliency in their daily lives. Stories can come from your personal experiences, from former students, from literature, or from short video clips. We don't want to simply tell kids to be resilient, we want to offer them specific tools and show them models of how resiliency impacts their daily lives.

◆ *Do some variation of "3 Things Thursdays"* – As a way to focus on gratitude and optimism, provide students with an opportunity to list and share the good things that are happening in their lives. Remember that good things can be both big (my family loves me) or small (I got to sit next to my best friend on the bus).

◆ *Use journals and writing tasks* – Allow students to explore concepts related to resiliency and stress management by way of low-stakes writing opportunities.

◆ *Use start statements* – When students are stressed, they'll often demonstrate unhealthy or inappropriate behaviors (just like adults). When we see misbehaviors in students, there is a tendency to tell them what to stop doing: stop worrying so much, stop wasting time, stop focusing so much on what other people are doing, etc. Rather than a constant barrage of the negative, use more *start* statements. These are positive, proactive statements or directions about what to begin rather than what to stop. For example, if you see a child exhibiting a nervous tic because they are worried about a test, give them a positive reframing statement or ask them to do something physical to take control of their body as a way to manage their anxiety. Shameless plug – for more information about start statements and other behavioral interventions, check out my book titled *75 Quick and Easy Solutions for Common Classroom Disruptions.*

◆ *Role-play* – Allow students to dive into concepts related to stress management and resiliency by way of role-playing, scenarios, and what if's. For example, don't wait to teach them how to manage conflict until they are in the middle of it. Be proactive.

◆ *Practice breathing and stretching* – Recall that stress is a perception of a lack of control. The best case scenario, when we are feeling stressed, is to gain control over the source of the stress. But that is not always possible. For students, that is *often* not possible. But, they can gain control over their bodies. Teach them how to breathe and how to stretch in order to gain a sense of control and calm.

◆ *Institute acts of required helpfulness* – As much as it might sound like an oxymoron, place students in situations where they are required to help each other. Helpfulness, it turns out, is beneficial not just for the person being helped. When we help someone else (and get positive feedback about it), we feel great about ourselves.

◆ *Ask, "What's the hard part?"* – When students are in the midst of a challenging situation, ask questions focused on getting them to identify and describe the situation. Helping someone build resiliency is often focused on helping them to isolate the issue and describe a possible solution.

4 Things Resilient Teachers
Hardly Ever Do

1

Resilient Teachers Hardly Ever Beat Themselves Up Over Past Mistakes

In a Nutshell: This chapter should be renamed "Resilient Teachers Hardly Ever *Spend Much Time* Beating Themselves Up Over Past Mistakes". The fact is, regardless of how resilient we've become, we all have those days where we look in mirror and say, "Ugh. What was I thinking?"

Digging Deeper: Before we dig deeper, let's pause for a moment. Based on what you know about being resilient (think about connections to stress and control), what is your response to the statement that *resilient teachers hardly every beat themselves up*? Why might this be true? Pause and reflect on that question for just a moment.

The primary reason that resilient teachers hardly ever spend much time beating themselves up over past mistakes is straightforward: the past cannot be controlled. In order to manage the stressors in my life, I need to have some control over something. The past, with all its mistakes, can be *learned from* but not controlled. If I spend too much time worrying or ruminating or feeling bad about how I've screwed up, I get depressed. That just leads to a deeper sense of helplessness. What I can do is recognize, apologize, and make amends. Those things are within my control.

Stress expert Robert Sapolsky (you've seen his name crop up several times throughout the book) puts it plainly, "Those who cope with stress successfully tend to seek control in the face of present stressors but do not try to control things that have already come to pass" (2004). He refers to "footholds of control"; small areas where we have influence that will allow us the tools to tackle larger problems.

It turns out that resilient people have an intimate, if not unique, relationship to failure. Resilient people find meaning from their failure and setbacks. In their book *The Resilience Factor* (2002), authors Karen Reivich and Andrew Shatte put it this way:

> Resilient people understand that failures are not an end point. They do not feel shame when they don't succeed. Instead resilient people are able to derive meaning from failure, and they use this knowledge to climb higher than they otherwise would.

Further, Dr. Glenn Schiraldi, in the *Resilience Workbook* (2017), reminds us that we cannot let our errors define us. If we do – if we live in the past and define our worth by past mistakes – we'll negate our true value, which may lead to a deeper sense of helplessness.

Every teacher has had a lesson where things went south – maybe in the middle of a lesson you realized you had no idea what you were talking about. Maybe you realized you gave wrong information or presented something unclearly. Maybe you had an "oh crap" moment where your principal entered the room during a rare moment you were checking your cell phone. In the classroom, most of us are pretty darn good most of the time, but we all have our moments. Resilience is how we respond when we've messed up; it includes both the way we think about the mistakes and what specific strategies we'll employ to help learn and move forward.

Within the research on resiliency, there is a lot written about concepts centered on the idea of self-forgiveness and self-compassion. To some, these concepts smack too much of pop-psychology, but there is tremendous power and control in recognizing your own humanity and freeing yourself from the bondage of guilt and shame. Rick Hanson, author of *Resilient - How to Grow an Unshakeable Core of Calm, Strength, and Happiness* (2018), speaks to the power of self-forgiveness. For some of us, it can often be more difficult to forgive ourselves than it is to forgive others. So, Hanson says to follow these steps: acknowledge that you blew it, take responsibility, do what is in your power to make amends and fix what you can, commit to not doing it again, and tell yourself that "You are forgiven".

Application Points

- ♦ *Remind yourself that no one is perfect* – No matter how resilient you've become, no one is perfect. That's a bit of a cliché, I know – *no one is perfect*. While it's true, it sometimes sounds trite. But nonetheless, when you've made mistakes and messed up, remind yourself that grace, patience, and forgiveness aren't just things that you grant to another person. Extend those to yourself as well. While not necessarily simple, it is essential to forgive yourself when you've messed up. You can't control the past, so don't live there.

- ♦ *Allow the emotion* – It is normal to feel embarrassed when we've messed up. In fact, if you don't feel some shade of guilt, there are probably larger issues. Remember that emotions are normal. Strong emotions, you may recall from our discussion in Chapter 5, is a way that your brain says, "Pay attention. We've got an issue". Give yourself permission to *feel the feels* but don't wallow. In fact, now might be a good time to go back and re-read Chapter 5.

- ♦ *Laugh* – My wife and I have some good friends at church, older friends who are in their 80s, who have adopted a great outlook on life's mistakes. They say, "At some point you are going to look back on this situation and laugh. You might as well start now".

- ♦ *Tame some voices* – Don't listen to certain voices in your head. In the chapter titled *Resilient Teachers Know their Triggers*, one of the application points was to "Recognize

ANTs". These are those automatic negative thoughts that sometimes creep into our thinking. Daniel and Tana Amen remind us that thoughts can lie and that not all thoughts need to be entertained.

◆ *Fail forward* – The concept is simple – when you've made a mistake, do your best to learn from it so that the next mistake (because there will be a *next* mistake) makes you better and keeps you working toward the goal of being a more effective teacher. The real question is this – are you making the *same* mistakes over and over?

◆ *Prepare some "pat" responses* – When immediately confronted with a mistake, error, or failure, have some ready-to-go phrases that you can tell yourself. Phrases like these may help to bring some perspective: "This was unplanned learning opportunity" or "This will help me to put Plan B into action". Note, these are internal conversations, not external ones. These are examples of self-talk to help work through the issue. If you use these phrases in your discussion with someone else, they could sound sarcastic or dismissive of the damage that may have been done to others.

◆ *Follow your own advice* – Imagine that you are counseling or advising someone who is working to overcome some mistakes. You'd probably give advice similar to what the Greater Good Science Center from the University of California at Berkeley suggests: (1) Be mindful, (2) Remember that you are not alone, and (3) Be kind to yourself. If those suggestions are good enough for other people, they are good enough for you, too.

2

Resilient Teachers Hardly Ever Spend Much Time Complaining

In a Nutshell: Grumbling about students, about the system, or about what should be is typically a waste of time. There is no perfect organization and the grass is rarely greener on the other side. Complaining and whining about problems typically adds more stress to life, not less.

Digging Deeper: Put plainly, a complaint is almost always focused on situations where we have no control. We complain about things like the wackiness of some parents, the decisions of leadership, or the behavior of our students – all things we cannot control. That, and complaining typically keeps us stuck in the past. That's a recipe for misery right there – a focus on things in the past that we cannot control.

Notice that I didn't say *"Resilient teachers spend zero time complaining"*. We all have bad days. No one is perfect and even the best of us sometimes fall victim to the frustrations of the job. The point is, to build resiliency and manage stress, we are better off focusing on those things we can control.

Even in the best of schools, there will be some negativity around you and some things that are genuinely wrong and should be fixed. Sometimes, that comes from colleagues; sometimes, it comes from administration; and sometimes, it comes from students and parents. If you find yourself feeding into that negativity, it will spread like a disease and infect just about every aspect of your life.

I'm not suggesting we all become Pollyannas who are overly positive and cheerful about everything regardless of how dire the situation is, but those things that I let occupy my mind will influence my behavior. What we focus on gets magnified in our thinking, which will ultimately influence behavior patterns. Because complaining about things is a thinking process, the more we do it, the more it can become ingrained and ultimately become a habit. In essence, complaining becomes a vicious cycle that can be hard to stop.

Part of the challenge in dealing with the negativity around us is the inevitable urge to make comparisons. Some research suggests that we spend up to 10% of our day comparing ourselves or our situations to something else (Summerville and Roese, 2008). A focus on comparisons will make you miserable, increase your stress levels, and lead to increase in pessimism (Deri et al., 2017). Teddy Roosevelt famously once said that, "comparison is the thief of joy". We should strive to find a balance between recognizing where we have influence (and asserting that influence appropriately) and where we need to let things go.

Application Points

  ◆ *What about venting?* – Venting can be a good thing but vent carefully and be cautious who you vent to. Also, keep the venting episodes short. Yet another reason you need to carefully select your mentors and friends is that not everyone can be trusted with your gripes and complaints. People gossip, and if you vent to the wrong people, it will likely cause an increase in your stress levels.

  ◆ *Quit your whining* – Isn't that what we tell kids – "*Quit your whinin' or I'll give you something to whine about*"? As previously mentioned, venting can be a good thing but recognize when you may have gone too far. Recognize when the thinking patterns have become destructive. Ask your trusted colleagues for feedback by posing questions such as "Do I complain about this too much?"

♦ *Challenge "if/only" thinking* – When we are frustrated, it's easy to fall into the "if/only" trap. We say things like "If we only had better parental support, we wouldn't have so many student behavior problems" or "If we only had more laptops, our students would be more engaged". While you may be right and have a valid concern, "if/only" thinking typically leads to more frustration.

♦ *Maintain perspective* – Remember that what you do makes a difference. In challenging or stressful times, remind yourself that you are a difference maker. In what other profession do you have the chance to daily impact a person's entire life?

♦ *Notice the small things* – Dr. Allen Mendler, in the wonderfully concise book *The Resilient Teacher*, challenges us to regularly focus on what goes right on any given day. Even on those days when the challenges are significant, there are enough things – sometimes small, unnoticed things – that go well: the custodian left the room in good condition, the air conditioning is working on a hot day, the cafeteria is serving your favorite food for lunch, or the principal visited the room when not a single student was having a meltdown. So, on a regular basis, simply take two to three minutes to brainstorm, and list those things that went well.

♦ *Review* – Reread Chapter 2 (gratitude) and Chapter 11 (focus on what you can control) to see how all the pieces of the puzzle fit together. While you are at it, take another look at the chapter titled *"Resilient Teachers Hardly Ever Beat Themselves Up Over Past Mistakes"*. You'll have some bad days, there is no doubt about that, but the more you get into the habit of forgiving yourself and then shifting what you think about, the more resilient you'll be.

♦ *But wait, I'm surrounded* – If you find yourself constantly around negative people who like to complain; if you find yourself in their lines of fire, here are some options:

  ♦ *Go to the bathroom* – Follow the advice of Annette Breaux (2015) who says that when you are cornered by a negative colleague who is attempting to "suck you into their sinkhole", make an excuse that you have to go to the bathroom. They probably won't follow you. If they do, you've got another set of problems.

◆ *Direct the conversation* – When you find yourself in a situation where the conversation turns negative (or is likely to turn negative), direct the conversation with questions that are more likely to elicit a positive response such as, "We have a 3-day weekend coming up, what fun thing do you have planned?". Or direct the conversation to something positive with a statement such as "You wouldn't believe the funny thing that one of my 3rd graders did this morning". At the very least, shift the conversation toward a neutral topic.

◆ *Avoid the staff lounge* – This is assuming that the staff lounge is where some of those negative colleagues congregate. If the staff lounge is a positive place that helps you recharge, by all means, hang out there. The idea is this – you have some choice and control where to spend your time. You are not stuck.

◆ *"Wait a minute, I am stuck"* – If that was your response to the previous statement, I get it. There are times when you are required to spend time with some less-than-positive colleagues. You might be required to participate in meetings or collaborate during a Professional Learning Community with them. In those cases where you really do feel stuck, here are some suggestions:

◆ Smile and remind yourself that you can't control anything but yourself and your own response.

◆ Be honest and vulnerable. Say, "I'm working really hard to stay positive in this situation because I don't want to become cynical. Let's change the discussion to focus on some solutions". Notice that the suggestion was not phrased as a question. Don't ask them if they would mind focusing on solutions. Don't say, "Please, let's be positive here". Instead, advocate for yourself and make statements, don't ask questions.

♦ If things get really bad or if negative situations persist, seek the advice and assistance of your administrator. It is their job to address things that negatively impact the culture of the school. While seeking the help of your administrator might not be your first line of offense, it shouldn't be your last. Don't wait until you are so frustrated that you are considering leaving before you talk with your principal.

3

Resilient Teachers Hardly Ever Freak Out About Change

In a Nutshell: Change is education is ubiquitous. Being resilient requires an understanding of the nature of change as well as which personal coping mechanisms are most helpful while in the midst of it.

Digging Deeper: Things change. Whether we like it or not, there is one thing you can count on year after year – stuff will change. You'll get a new curriculum right when we were feeling proficient with the current one, new standards will be developed that seem confusing or unnecessary, leadership will change and new colleagues will come aboard, and we'll get new students who will bring ever-increasing needs. Being resilient requires a way to think about the changes we face as well as a set of coping mechanisms when the changes seem difficult to manage.

We'll start this chapter by reminding you of a few things you likely already know about change:

- ◆ It's inevitable and normal.
- ◆ Some people like it, some people don't.
- ◆ Some change is easy, some change is difficult.
- ◆ It is easier to coach someone else through change than to coach yourself.
- ◆ There are often strong emotions that accompany a call for change.

♦ It is hard to change when you are under a lot of stress (Neal et al., 2013).

♦ If we don't accept change, we're hypocrites. After all, every day we ask our students to embrace new knowledge, try new skills, and step out of their comfort zones. When we refuse to do the same, it looks pretty bad and we lose credibility.

♦ We may accept change, but if we do it with a lousy attitude, we're still hypocrites. After all, every day we ask our students to embrace new knowledge, try new skills, and step out of their comfort zones *and do so with a positive attitude*.

♦ Changes can be "exciting in principle" but more challenging to put into practice. When we hear about new initiatives or new programs, the theory can make sense while we are sitting in a training workshop, but hard to implement once we are in the classroom (Fisher et al., 2012).

♦ Our brains quickly and unconsciously form opinions about proposed changes. We like to think of ourselves as being objective about change but our experiences and subjective interpretations influence our thinking (Wilson, 2011).

Let's remember what Spencer Johnson taught us in the classic book *Who Moved My Cheese?* If you are not familiar with the book, here is a quick summary: it is a story of four characters – Sniff, Scurry, Hem and Haw – who live in a maze and search for cheese. Sniff and Scurry are mice, and Hem and Haw are little people. The story begins as the four of them set out in search of cheese. In the story, cheese represents what we want, value, or long for in life. For some of us, cheese is financial stability; for others, it is a certain type of relationship; and for others, it might be obtaining a job or a college degree. One day the four characters found a huge supply of cheese and they were happy and content, having found what they searched for. But, as you might imagine based on the title of the book, one day, they found that someone had moved their cheese; it was all gone. As an allegory of change, the story follows the process that each character goes through to adapt and respond to that change. Sniff and Scurry responded quickly and adapt well. It takes some time (and frustration and sleepless nights and worry) for Haw to fully realize that change has taken place and that he must respond. We never find out how Hem ultimately responds to the change. Dr. Johnson leaves that up to the reader to decide.

The story of *Who Moved My Cheese?* focuses primarily on the character of Haw. As he works through the emotions and challenges of accepting the fact that his cheese had been moved, he comes to several realizations. He writes these insights on the walls of the maze to help him remember and to hopefully encourage his friend Hem (who did not handle the cheese relocation very well). Here are some of those insights from Haw: *If you do not change, you become extinct; What would you do if you weren't afraid?; Movement in a new direction helps you to find new cheese; The quicker you let go of old cheese, the sooner you'll find new cheese.* Being resilient is recognizing that change is going to happen; your cheese is going to be moved whether you like it or not. The sooner we recognize and accept that change is simply a normal and inevitable part of our profession, the better off we are. And, when we take control of our response to that change, we are practicing resilience.

If change is a constant – if it is normal and inevitable that my cheese is going to be moved – why do I say that resilient teachers *hardly ever freak out* about it? Well, no one is perfect and change often involves an emotional response. Even the most resilient of us sometimes respond with, *"Oh, geez. Seriously? What in the world are they thinking? This is crazy and stupid and unnecessary!"* Regardless of how unafraid we might be about tackling change, there are simply times when a change is forced upon us when we really don't see the need for it. We don't always respond as appropriately as we should. The difference is that resilient teachers don't stay stuck in a negative mindset for long (Dweck, 2006).

Sometimes, the changes we are confronted with are unfair, undeserved, or forced upon us. I know it's a cliché, but it is also true – *life is unfair*. The truth is that life is *negatively* unfair at times and *positively* unfair at times. When something negative forces a change upon us, we often label that unfair. You might lose a job, get sick, have horrible neighbors move in next door, or have an ungrateful child rebel against you. We could tally up those times in our lives when something bad happened that we didn't deserve. That is the essence of unfairness; when you get something you don't deserve.

We can also view unfairness from another perspective. We can also tally up those times in life when we received something positive that we didn't deserve. Maybe it was an unexpected monetary gift that helped you get through a tough time, maybe it was being forgiven after you've done something unkind, or maybe it was as simple as having the person in front of you in line pay for your coffee. Consider some of the synonyms of the word unfair: *unwarranted, unequal, unjust, undue.* It is easy to define those words in a negative way, but we can also think of them as positives. Grace, mercy, favor, courtesy, and forgiveness are all unfair as well.

As a practical exercise, do what UCLA psychiatrist Dr. Stephen Marmer suggests: compare the undeserved good against the undeserved bad. For most of us, the good far outweighs the bad. Doing this does not dismiss or trivialize the bad things that have happened to you, it simply helps to put it into perspective. Dealing with change, particularly unwanted change, is all about perspective.

Application Points

♦ *Model how to think about change* – Show your students specific thinking patterns and coping mechanisms when faced with a need to change. Dr. Eric Jensen suggests that we help students identify headwinds and tailwinds. Headwinds are those things in life that make the pedaling or rowing just a bit harder; the wind is in your face slowing you down. Tailwinds are those things that assist, push, and aide your journey. Everyone has both tailwinds and headwinds. When we recognize and call upon those supports that help us to keep going, we are being resilient.

- *Do a quick review* – Go back and review the chapters on gratitude, reframing, how to manage emotions, in-the-moment stress relievers, and professional support networks. Remind yourself of the information and skills you've learned throughout this book.
- *Acknowledge emotions* – Recognizing an emotional reaction to a change is the first important step.
- *Seek help* – Reach out to mentors, coaches, and trusted colleagues. When faced with change, seek their wisdom and advice in order to help bring things into perspective. Ask them, "How am I responding to this situation?" or "Help me see this change from a different perspective".
- *Find small positive things* – Martin Seligman, who is often referred to as the founder of the positive psychology movement, conducted a study in 2005 in which participants were asked to write down three good things that happened to them each day (plus the causes of the good things). They were asked to do this every day for a week – recognize and write down both big and small things that happened to them that were positive. The results – participants reported an increase in happiness and a decrease in depression *that lasted for six months.*
- *Self-reflect* – In the midst of a change that you may not want to fully accept, stop and consider on what are you focusing your thoughts. Ask, "Is this thinking pattern helping me or harming me?" or "Are these ruminations keeping me stuck or helping me find a way to move forward?"
- *Self-reflect some more* – Elena Aguilar, in the book *Onward: Cultivating Emotional Resilience in Educators*, suggests the following exercise: finish this sentence in multiple ways, "Change is…".
- *Ask, what is the change really all about?* – Realize that most of the proposed changes in our profession focus more on implementation of strategies and approaches than they do foundational, core values. Most changes focus more on the way things are done and less on what needs to be done. For example, you may share the core belief with

your principal that character education is essential. That core belief is not likely to change. What may change are the programs, curricula, and methods we go about supporting character education.

♦ *Remember, change is just about learning* – You can learn anything you need to learn. It just takes commitment and time. When we view the change as simply the need to learn a new set of skills, a new approach, or a new idea, it can become empowering. After all, most teachers profess a love for learning. This mindset – that change is simply getting to learn something new – puts that love for learning into action.

♦ *Expect barriers* – Even when you've got a good attitude about the change and you have good supports (tailwinds), there will almost always be roadblocks and unexpected obstacles. Don't be surprised when things get bumpy. It's normal; things rarely go as smoothly as we had hoped. Resiliency has been described as a person's internal shock absorbers. Just like a car's ride is smoother when there are shock absorbers, life is smoother when we practice resiliency. Shock absorbers don't remove the bumps in the road; they make them easier to navigate.

♦ *Remember Haw* – In *Who Moved My Cheese?*, Haw discovered that when he was able to laugh at himself (for taking so long to begin searching for new cheese) and when he was able to focus on what he'll get instead of what he lost, he felt empowered to search for new cheese.

♦ *Imagine the future* – Picture a positive future in which you've mastered the new skill or overcome the current challenge. Part of being resilient is realizing that nothing lasts forever. The frustration or irritation that you might be feeling is temporary. Allow yourself to daydream and imagine how great you'll feel when the current situation is under control.

4

Resilient Teachers Hardly Ever Shy Away from Conflict

In a Nutshell: Conflict is normal, expected, inevitable, and healthy. Clarification – *the right kind* of conflict is healthy. Resilient people don't wish for conflict, but they have the skills, mindsets, and coping mechanisms to deal with it effectively.

Digging Deeper: I am convinced of this one very important truth: the world would be a much better place if we all accepted the fact that conflict is a natural and unavoidable part of life. In order to deal with conflict in a professional and effective way, we first need to understand the nature of it; as educators, we must have a solid grasp of what conflict is and how it is likely to manifest itself in the school setting. We must also have practical coping mechanisms to use when we find ourselves in the middle of it.

If you have no conflict in your life, one of two things is true: you're dead or you're not paying attention to the people around you. Since you are reading this, let's start with the latter. Whenever you interact with the people around you – whether they be family members, co-workers, friends, or a stranger at the store, there is the possibility (or rather the *likelihood*) that conflict will arise. If you look up dictionary definitions, you'll find phrases like *struggle for power*, *strong disagreement*, and *an opposition of forces*. None of those are pleasant, so it's no wonder people strive to avoid conflict.

However, conflict is simply a by-product of being around other people. That is one of the first things that resilient people understand – conflict simply is. It exists because I interact with other people. Its existence does not make me a bad person nor does it necessarily mean that I am doing something wrong (although my responses can often make the situation much, much worse). Too often, we assign blame, place guilt upon ourselves, or ignore conflict when it arises. None of those are healthy responses.

So, what exactly is conflict and where does it come from? In terms of external conflict with other people, conflict typically comes from one of three situations: *blocked goals or expectations*, *opposing beliefs or points of view*, or *miscommunication*. In the simplest terms, someone has something I want = conflict. Someone is in my way = conflict. Someone thinks or says something I don't like = conflict. Someone communicates in a way I don't understand or appreciate = bingo, conflict!

For our purposes here, we'll distill down to some basic, foundational understandings of conflict. In reality, the study of conflict is varied, deep, and nuanced, but there are some easy-to-understand concepts that we can quickly put into practice without having to spend months researching the topic. In summary, here are some big truths about conflict:

- **It is** – As I mentioned before, conflict is just a natural part of the human existence. Its presence in my life merely means that I am interacting with other flawed, imperfect people.
- **It is unavoidable, expect it** – I should not be surprised, flabbergasted, or stunned when I find myself in conflict with someone. Nor should I be overly frustrated.
- **It can be a good thing** – The right kind of conflict can serve as a catalyst for personal growth. Don't get me wrong, few people love conflict, but when it is handled correctly, we can learn a lot about ourselves and the people around us.
- **Expect common reactions** – Conflict is an emotional thing for most of us, so we shouldn't be surprised when

see or experience these typical reactions: competition, compromise, avoidance, complaining, collaboration, and accommodation (Thomas and Kilmann, 1978). Some of those reactions are healthy, some are not. But they are all normal and to be expected.

◆ **Conflict cues the brain** – Our brains respond in very specific ways when we are confronted with conflict. Since our brain's basic function is to ensure our survival, when we sense conflict, we shift into survival mode. Among other things, chemicals like cortisol and dopamine are released and the Ventral Tegmental area of the brain hyper-focuses attention and monitors the conflict (Mamiya et al., 2020). This may help to explain why we spend so much time worrying, thinking, and ruminating when we are in conflict. Quite simply, for most of us, conflict is stressful and evokes emotions which trigger the brain to focus on survival.

◆ **It can be healthy or unhealthy** – Allen Amason, a researcher who studies strategic change, has identified two different kinds of conflict: affective and cognitive. Affective conflict focuses on feelings, past experiences, emotions, and typically centers on people or events. Cognitive conflict, on the other hand, focuses on ideas, issues, or processes. As you can probably guess, one of these is healthy, one is not. One of these will help you to grow and improve, while the other will keep you stuck. The "In a Nutshell" statement at the beginning of the chapter indicated that *the right kind* of conflict is a good thing. That's cognitive conflict. You actually want to have cognitive conflict in your life. You want to interact with people who challenge your ideas and push you to improve. When we disagree but stay focused on the issues, we become better. When we disagree but stay focused on our feelings, we rarely get better. For example, you may be working with a group of colleagues on ways to improve the formative assessment process at your school. If you spend time disagreeing about ideas or the best methods to accomplish the goals, you'll likely be productive.

However, if you spend time disagreeing because you don't particularly like the people you are working with, you won't get far. Cognitive conflict focuses on *the what, the why, and the how* to get things done. Affective conflict focuses on the people, the emotions, and prior offenses. We see examples of people confusing and mixing the two types of conflict all the time. Take politics, for example. Rarely do politicians truly listen to each other and focus on ideas. What happens far too often is that they disregard the ideas and suggestions of others simply because they don't like previous political stances or what label the other person has chosen (i.e., democrat v republican v independent).

The next time you find yourself in conflict, here are five easy steps to help work through it: **First**, identify the type of conflict you are experiencing. Is it affective or cognitive? Are you focusing on people and feelings and past offenses or are you focusing on ideas and concepts. The truth is that we often mix the two without realizing it. It can be very easy to disregard really good ideas because you don't particularly like the source of those ideas. If we do that, if we disregard ideas because we don't like the person or organization the ideas are coming from, we miss out on lots of ways we can improve and get better.

Second, make sure to spend time listening and gathering as much information as you can about the issue in front of you. Without all the facts, it is hard to make good decisions. Remember what Stephen Covey taught us – *seek first to understand, then to be understood*. **Third**, in very specific terms, define the issue(s) you are facing. After you have listened and gathered facts, turn around and do your best to concretely define what it is that you have to change, do, create, or consider. We often find ourselves in conflict because we are being asked to do something differently. Make sure that you can clearly define the issue in front of you. If you cannot, go back and listen some more, ask questions, and seek the advice of a trusted mentor or colleague. The **fourth** step is to rate, on a scale of 1–10, your understanding of the issues, changes, or conflicts you are facing. When we attach a number to an abstract situation, it can help to clarify things. For example, answer this question, *"On a scale of 1–10, how clear are you about the next steps you need to take to implement this new idea?"* A relatively high rating means that you may be ready to take action; a relatively low rating may mean that it is time to go back to steps 1 or 2. In all reality, steps 3 and 4 go hand in hand. They provide tools to help bring clarity to the conflict because you cannot help to resolve a conflict that you don't understand.

Finally, the **fifth** step is to take action. Remember the relationship between stress and control; when we take control by taking action, we reduce our stress levels. Based on what you learned about the conflict (and about yourself) during the first four steps, decide what actions need to be taken. These steps help us to become adept at dealing with conflict.

Before you dig in to the specific application points related to conflict, go back and review the previous chapter titled *"Resilient Teachers Hardly Ever Freak Out about Change"*. Look for commonalities of ideas and concepts and note that many of the applications work here as well. Change and conflict often go hand in hand; they both involve strong emotions and force us to be introspective about the situations we face.

Application Points

- ◆ *Quit taking it personally (QTIP)* is a powerful mindset. Other peoples' behavior typically says more about them than it does about you. When students or colleagues act in inappropriate ways, it is not usually about us (unless, of course, it is about us because we haven't responded in the most appropriate ways).
- ◆ *Don't catastrophize, exaggerate, or trivialize* – When in the midst of conflict, it doesn't help to go to extremes. Remember that there are likely strong emotions involved and rarely does it help to downplay or dismiss those strong emotions.
- ◆ *Avoid pronouns* – When we use terms like *I, they, us, we,* and *them*, we automatically pit people and groups against each other. It is best to stick to the facts when describing

a situation that needs to be addressed. Although others may use lots of pronouns as they describe their conflict, we can help lower the stress levels of all involved if we remain neutral in our language.

◆ *Avoid sarcasm* – Sarcasm will always make the situation worse. Period.

◆ *Don't be surprised* – As educators, we should not be surprised or upset when our students or our colleagues are in conflict. The fact is that many of our students are not learning effective conflict resolution skills at home and there aren't a ton of excellent examples of conflict resolution models in the media, sports, entertainment, or politics.

◆ *Respond rather than react* – Remember that conflict is a natural result of people spending time together. Schools and classrooms are unique places – lots of people crammed together in a confined space for long periods of time. That's practically a recipe for conflict. So, it's not a matter of *if* there will be problems, it's a matter of when and how often. As teachers and leaders, our job is to respond with a thoughtful plan.

◆ *Embody respect* – In some cases, we may be the best role models our students or colleagues have. As a result, we must always embody respect, show empathy, and express appreciation for everyone. Quite simply, we must be good role models. Think about the message we are sending to kids if we get easily offended, outright mad, start yelling, or demean those around us.

◆ *Embody empathy* – Regarding any situation or conflict you are facing, consider that you are rarely 100% right and the other person or group is 100% wrong. Even if you are completely in the right, do your best to remember what it was like the last time you were the one who was 100% wrong. Grace and forgiveness go a long way in managing conflict. A bias toward empathy and forgiveness also helps us to manage our ego and emotions.

◆ *Separate the person from the problem* – Recall the differences between affective and cognitive conflict. We do best when we are able to separate the issues from the personalities. More time spent focusing on issues, the better off we are.

◆ *Be quick* – Deal with conflict or difficult issues quickly and honestly; don't let difficult situations or possible conflicts fester. Heed the advice of your dentist – rarely do problems get better by ignoring them. Often, procrastination or avoidance hurts *us* more than anyone else. Worrying, fretting, and complaining typically take more of a toll on you than it does on anyone else.

◆ *Teach students* – Use role-plays, scenarios, current events, and other real-life situations to teach students the appropriate ways to handle conflict. Our students need and deserve to learn these skills, but we cannot wait until "the heat of the moment" to try to talk kids through the process. Again, it's not a matter of *if* there will be conflict in your classroom, it's a matter of when. So, get ahead of the curve and incorporate teaching opportunities throughout the school year.

What's Next?

Throughout this book, you've considered 21 methods to build resiliency and manage stress. You've also taken a look at over 275 specific application points. Perhaps, it's been a bit like drinking from a fire hose – a lot of great information that can be overwhelming at times. To help consider which of those ideas and applications are most immediately useful and relevant, use the form below to organize your thoughts.

1. **Resilient Teachers Take Care of Their Health**

   Application Points:

   _____

   _____

   _____

   Notes & Questions:

   _____

   _____

   _____

2. **Resilient Teachers Practice Gratitude**

   Application Points:

   _____

   _____

   _____

   Notes & Questions:

   _____

   _____

   _____

3. Resilient Teachers Practice Reframing

Application Points:

_____

_____

_____

Notes & Questions:

_____

_____

_____

4. Resilient Teachers Understand the Power of "No"

Application Points:

_____

_____

_____

Notes & Questions:

_____

_____

_____

5. Resilient Teachers Manage Their Emotions

Application Points:

_____

_____

_____

Notes & Questions:

_____

_____

_____

6. **Resilient Teachers Know Their Triggers**

   Application Points:

   _____

   _____

   _____

   Notes & Questions:

   _____

   _____

   _____

7. **Resilient Teachers Practice In-The-Moment Stress Relievers**

   Application Points:

   _____

   _____

   _____

   Notes & Questions:

   _____

   _____

   _____

8. **Resilient Teachers Develop a Professional Support Network**

   Application Points:

   _____

   _____

   _____

   Notes & Questions:

   _____

_____

_____

9. Resilient Teachers Have a Life Outside the Classroom

Application Points:

_____

_____

_____

Notes & Questions:

_____

_____

_____

10. Resilient Teachers Get Themselves Organized

Application Points:

_____

_____

_____

Notes & Questions:

_____

_____

_____

11. Resilient Teachers Focus on What They Can Control

Application Points:

_____

_____

_____

Notes & Questions:

_____

_____

_____

12. Resilient Teachers Know How to Receive Feedback

Application Points:

_____

_____

_____

Notes & Questions:

_____

_____

_____

13. Resilient Teachers Advocate for Themselves

Application Points:

_____

_____

_____

Notes & Questions:

_____

_____

_____

14. Resilient Teachers Create and Track Goals

Application Points:

_____

_____

_____

Notes & Questions:

_____

_____

_____

15. Resilient Teachers Unplug

Application Points:

_____

_____

_____

Notes & Questions:

_____

_____

_____

16. Resilient Teachers Laugh and Have Fun With Their Students

Application Points:

_____

_____

_____

Notes & Questions:

_____

_____

_____

17. **Resilient Teachers Help Students Build Resiliency**

Application Points:

_____

_____

_____

Notes & Questions:

_____

_____

_____

1. **Resilient Teachers Hardly Ever Beat Themselves Up Over Past Mistakes**

Application Points:

_____

_____

_____

Notes & Questions:

_____

_____

_____

2. **Resilient Teachers Hardly Ever Spend Much Time Complaining**

Application Points:

_____

_____

_____

Notes & Questions:

_____

_____

_____

3. Resilient Teachers Hardly Ever Freak Out About Change

Application Points:

_____

_____

_____

Notes & Questions:

_____

_____

_____

4. Resilient Teachers Hardly Ever Shy Away From Conflict

Application Points:

_____

_____

_____

Notes & Questions:

_____

_____

_____

References

Abbass, A. (March, 2005). Somatization: Diagnosing it sooner through emotion-focused interviewing. *The Journal of Family Practice*, 54(3), 215.

Aguilar, E. (2018). *Onward – Cultivating Emotional Resilience in Educators*. San Francisco, CA: John Wiley & Sons.

Ahdoot, R. (2016). *Sarcasm RULES*. Retrieved from https://www.smartbrief.com/original/2016/01/sarcasm-rules.

Allen, S. E. (2009). *Future-Mindedness*. A white paper prepared for the John Templeton Foundation, Greater Good Science Center, UC Berkeley.

Altman, E. M. (2017). Comparing switch costs: Alternating runs and explicit cuing. *Journal of Experimental Psychology: Learning, Memory, and Cognition*, 33(3), 475–483.

Amason, A., Mooney, A., & Holahan, P. (2007). Don't take it personally: Exploring cognitive conflict as a mediator of affective conflict. *Journal of Management Studies*, 44(5), 733–758. First published: 19 February 2007. DOI: 10.1111/j.1467-6486.2006.00674.x

Amen, D. (2005). *Making a Good Brain Great*. New York: Harmony Books.

Amen, D., & Amen, T. (2016). *The Brain Warrior's Way*. New York: New American Library Press.

Anderson, M. (2010). *The Well-Balanced Teacher*. Alexandria, VA: ASCD.

Banas, J., Dunbar, N., Rodriguez, D., & Liu, S. (2011). A review of humor in educational settings: Four decades of research. *Communication Education*, 60(1), 115–144. DOI: 10.1080/03634523.2010.496867

Bandura, A. (1997). *Self-Efficacy – The Exercise of Control*. New York: W.H. Freeman and Company.

Bender, W. (2015). *20 Disciplinary Strategies for Working with Challenging Students*. West Palm Beach, FL: Learning Sciences International.

Berk, L. (2006). Anticipating a laugh reduces our stress hormones, study shows. *ScienceDaily*, 10 April 2008.

Breaux, A. (2015). Ten things master teachers do. *ASCD Express*, 10(23).

Burzynska, A., Wong, C., Voss, M., Cooke, G., Gothe, N., Fanning, J., McAuley, E., & Kramer, A. (2015). Physical activity is linked to greater moment-to-moment variability in spontaneous brain activity in older adults. *PLoS One*, 10(8), e0134819. DOI: 10.1371/journal.pone.0134819

Chae, B., & Rui, S. (2014). Environmental disorder leads to self-regulatory failure. *Journal of Consumer Research*, 40(6), 1203–1218.

Cohen, S., Janicki-Deverts, D., Turner, R. B., & Doyle, W. J. (2015). Does hugging provide stress-buffering social support? A study of susceptibility to upper respiratory infection and illness. *Psychological Science*, 26(2), 135–147. DOI: 10.1177/0956797614559284

Covey, S. (1989). *The 7 Habits of Highly Effective People*. Kottayam: DC Books.

Craig, S. (2016). *Trauma-Sensitive Schools*. New York: Teachers College Press.

Culbertson, R. (2012). *Do It Well – Make It Fun*. Austin, TX: Greenleaf Book Group Press.

Davison, K. M., Lin, S. L., Tong, H., Kobayashi, K. M., Mora-Almanza, J. G., & Fuller-Thomson, E. (2020). Nutritional factors, physical health and immigrant status are associated with anxiety disorders among middle-aged and older adults: Findings from baseline data of The Canadian Longitudinal Study on Aging (CLSA). *International Journal of Environment and Research Public Health*, 17, 1493.

Deri, S., Davidai, S., & Gilovich, T. (2017). Home alone: Why people believe others' social lives are richer than their own. *Journal of Personality and Social Psychology*, 113(6), 858–877. DOI: 10.1037/pspa0000105

DeSteno, D., Li, Y., Dickens, L., & Lerner, J. (2014). Gratitude: A tool for reducing Economic Impatience. *Psycological Science*, 25(6), 1262–1267. DOI: 10.1177/0956797614529979

Dewall, N. (March, 2012). A grateful heart is a nonviolent heart: Cross-sectional, experience sampling, longitudinal, and experimental evidence. *Social Psychological and Personality Science*, 3(2), 232–240. DOI: 10.1177/1948550611416675

Dweck, C. (2006). *Mindset*. New York: Random House.

Dweck, C. (2016). *From the Learning and the Brain Conference*, Keynote address.

Emmons, R. A., & McCullough, M. E. (2003). Counting blessings versus burdens: An experimental investigation of gratitude and subjective well-being in daily life. *Journal of Personality and Social Psychology*, 84, 377–389.

Fisher, D., Frey, N., & Pumpian, I. (2012). *How to Create a Culture of Achievement in Your School and Classroom*. Alexandria, VA: ASCD.

Fleming, A. (2006). Positive psychology "three good things in life" and measuring happiness, positive and negative affectivity, optimism/hope, and well-being. *Counselor Education Master's Theses*, 32. Retrieved from http://digitalcommons.brockport.edu/edc_theses/32

Flook, L., Goldberg, S. B., Pinger, L., Bonus, K., & Davidson, R. J. (2013). Mindfulness for teachers: A pilot study to assess effects on stress, burnout, and teaching efficacy. *Mind, Brain, and Education*, 7, 182–195. DOI: 10.1111/mbe.12026

Frankl, V. (1984). *Man's Search for Meaning*. New York: Touchstone.

Gardener, H., Wright, C. B., Dong, C., Cheung, K., DeRosa, J., Nannery, M., Stern, Y., Elkind, M. S. V., & Sacco, R. L. (2016). Ideal cardiovascular health and cognitive aging in the Northern Manhattan Study. *Journal of the American Heart Association*, 5, e002731.

Gibson, M., & Shrader, J. (2014). Time use and productivity: The wage returns to sleep. Retrieved from https://online.wsj.com/public/resources/documents/091814sleep.pdf

Gino, F. (2015). *The Surprising Benefits of Sarcasm*. Retrieved from https://www.scientificamerican.com/article/the-surprising-benefits-of-sarcasm/

Godin, S. (2009). *The Thing About Goals*. Retrieved from https://seths.blog/2009/01/the-thing-about/

Goleman, D. (1995). *Emotional Intelligence*. New York: Bantam.

Goodwin, T. (2018). *Off: The Digital Detox to a Better Life*. New York: Harry N. Abrams.

Grant, A., Curtayne, L., & Burton, G. (2009). Executive coaching enhances goal attainment, resilience and workplace well-being: A randomised controlled study. *Journal of Positive Psychology*, 4(5), 396–407. DOI: 10.1080/17439760902992456

Grant, A. M., & Gino, F. (2010). A little thanks goes a long way: Explaining why gratitude expressions motivate prosocial behavior. *Journal of Personality and Social Psychology*, 98(6), 946–955. DOI: 10.1037/a0017935

Gross, J., and John, O. (2003). Individual differences in two emotion regulation processes: Implications for affect, relationships, and well-being. *Journal of Personality and Social Psychology*, 85, 348–362. DOI: 10.1037/0022–3514.85.2.348

Hammer, M. D. (2005). Rejuvenating retirees: Mentoring first-year teachers. *Delta Kappa Gamma Bulletin*, 71(4), 20–25.

Hanson, R. (2018). *Resilient – How to Grow and Unshakable Core of Calm, Strength, and Happiness*. New York: Harmony Books.

Harris, B. (2015). *Retaining New Teachers*. Alexandria, VA: ASCD.

Hart, W., & Albarracín, D. (2009). The effects of chronic achievement motivation and achievement primes on the activation of achievement and fun goals. *Journal of Personality and Social Psychology*, 97(6), 1129–1141. DOI: 10.1037/a0017146

Hartling, L. (2008). Strengthening resilience in a risky world: It's all about relationships. *Women & Therapy*, 31, 2–4, 51–70. DOI: 10.1080/02703140802145870

Heen, S., & Douglas, D. (2017). *Find the Coaching in Criticism in Emotional Intelligence: Resilience*. Boston, MA: Harvard Business Review Press.

Hirotsu, C., Tufik, S., & Andersen, M. L. (2015). Interactions between sleep, stress, and metabolism: From physiological to pathological conditions. *Sleep Science (Sao Paulo, Brazil)*, 8(3), 143–152. DOI: 10.1016/j.slsci.2015.09.002

Holt-Lunstad, J., Smith, T. B., & Layton, J. B. (2010). Social relationships and mortality risk: A meta-analytic review. *PLoS Medicine*, 7(7), e1000316. DOI: 10.1371/journal.pmed.1000316

Jensen, E. (2005). *Teaching with the Brain in Mind*. Alexandria, VA: ASCD.

Jensen, E. *The Importance of the Impossible*. https://www.jensenlearning.com/news/the-importance-of-the-impossible/brain-based-teaching

Johnson, S. (1998). *Who Moved My Cheese*. New York: Putnam.

Jones, P. (2017). *Exactly What to Say – The Magic Words for Influence and Impact*. Page Two Books.

Kansas State University. (2009). Psychologists show that future-minded people make better decisions for their health. *ScienceDaily*. Retrieved April 23, 2020 from www.sciencedaily.com/releases/2009/12/091223125129.htm

Kleon, A. (2019). *Keep Going: 10 Ways to Stay Creative in Good Times and Bad*. New York: Workman Publishing.

Levitin, D. (2020). *Successful Aging*. New York: Dutton Press.

Li, M., & Nishikawa, T. (2012). The relationship between active coping and trait resilience across U.S. and Taiwanese college student samples. *Journal of College Counseling*, 15, 157–171. DOI: 10.1002/j.2161-1882.2012.00013.x

Mamiya, P., Richards, T., Corrigan, M., & Kuhl, P. (2020). Strength of ventral tegmental area connections with left caudate nucleus is related to conflict monitoring. *Frontiers Psychology*, 10, 2869. DOI: 10.3389/fpsyg.2019.02869. eCollection 2019.

Mansfield, C., Beltman, S., & Price, A. (2014). 'I'm coming back again!' The resilience process of early career teachers. *Teachers and Teaching*, 20, 1–21. DOI: 10.1080/13540602.2014.937958.

Marano, H. E. (2003). The art of resilience. *Psychology Today*, May 1, 2003.

Margolis, J., & Stoltz, P. (2018). How to bounce back from adversity. In on mental toughness. *Harvard Business Review*, 88(1/2).

Matthews, D., & Clark, C. (1999). *The Faith Factor*. Middlesex: Penguin Books.

Maxwell, J. (2007). *Failing Forward: Turning Mistakes into Stepping Stones for Success*.

Mayer, J., & Salovey, P. (1997). What is emotional intelligence? In P. Salovey & D. J. Sluyter (Eds.), *Emotional Development and Emotional Intelligence: Educational Implications* (pp. 3–34). New York: Harper Collins.

McCullough, M., Tsang, J., & Emmons, R. (2004). Gratitude in intermediate affective terrain: Links of grateful moods to individual differences and daily emotional experience. *Journal of Personality and Social Psychology*, 86(2), 295–309.

Medea, B., Karapanagiotidis, T., Konishi, M., et al. (2018). How do we decide what to do? Resting-state connectivity patterns and components of self-generated thought linked to the development of more concrete personal goals. *Experimental Brain Research*, 236, 2469–2481. DOI: 10.1007/s00221-016-4729-y

Medina, J. (2008). *Brain Rules*. Seattle, WA: Pear Press.

Mendler, A. (2014). *The Resilient Teacher*. Alexandria, VA: ASCD.

Miller, E., & Cohen, J. (2001). An integrative theory of prefrontal cortex function. *Annual Review of Neuroscience*, 24, 167–202.

Mindup Curriculum. (2011). *Brain-Focused Strategies for Learning and Living*. New York: Scholastic Teaching Resources.

Nagasaki, E., & Nagaski, A. (2019). *Burnout: The Secret to Unlocking the Stress Cycle*. New York: Ballantine Press.

National Institute of Health. (2013). *The Benefits of Slumber – Why You Need a Good Night's Sleep*. Greenville, PA.

Neal, D., Wood, W., & Drolet, A. (2013). How do people adhere to goals when willpower is low? The profits (and pitfalls) of strong habits. *Journal of Personality and Social Psychology*, 104(6), 959–975.

Oberle, E., & Schonert-Reichl, K. (2016). Stress contagion in the classroom? The link between classroom teacher burnout and morning cortisol in elementary school students. *Social Science Medicine*, 159, 30–37. DOI: 10.1016/j.socscimed.2016.04.031. Epub 2016 April 24.

O'Connell, B., O'Shea, D., & Gallagher, S. (2017). Feeling thanks and saying thanks: A randomized controlled trial examining if and how socially oriented gratitude journals work. *Journal of Clinical Psychology*, 73, 1280–1300. DOI: 10.1002/jclp.22469

Oliver, G., Wardle, J., & Leigh, G. (2000). Stress and food choice: A laboratory study. *Psychosomatic Medicine*, 62(6), 853–865.

Orehek, E., & Inagaki, T. (2017). On the benefits of giving social support: When, why, and how support providers gain by caring for others. *Current Directions in Psychological Science*, 26, 109–113.

Osman, M. (2014). *Future-Minded: The Psychology of Agency and Control*. London: Red Globe Press.

Pasricha, N. (2016). *The Happiness Equation*. New York: G.P. Putnam's Sons.

Provine, R. (2004). Laughing, tickling, and the evolution of speech and self. *Current Directions in Psychological Science*, 13(6), 215–218. DOI: 10.1111/j.0963-7214.2004.00311.x

Reivich, K., & Shatte, A. (2002). *The Resilience Factor*. New York: Broadway Books.

Richards, K., Levesque-Bristol, C., Templin, T., & Graber, K. (2016). The impact of resilience on role stressors and burnout in elementary and secondary teachers. *Social Psychology of Education*, 19(3), 511–536. DOI: 10.1007/s11218-016-9346-x

Saks, A. (1994). Moderating effects of self-efficacy for the relationship between training method and anxiety and stress reactions of newcomers. *Journal of Organizational Behavior*, 15, 639–654. DOI: 10.1002/job.4030150707

Sapolsky, R. (2004). *Why Zebras Don't Get Ulcers*. New York: St. Martin's Griffin.

Schiraldi, G. (2017). *The Resilience Workbook*. Oakland, CA: New Harbinger Publications.

Schiraldi, G., Jackson, T., Brown, S., & Jordan, J. (2010). Resilience training for functioning adults. *International Journal of Emergency Mental Health*, 12, 117–129.

Schultchen, D., Reichenberger, J., Mittl, T., Weh, T., Smyth, J. M., Blechert, J., & Pollatos, O. (2019). Bidirectional relationship of stress and affect with physical activity and healthy eating. *British Journal of Health Psychology*, 24(2), 315–333. DOI: 10.1111/bjhp.12355

Schwartz, T. (2011). *Whatever You Feel Compelled to Do, Don't.* https://hbr.org/2011/05/whatever-you-feel-compelled-to.html

Seligman, M., & Steen, T. (2005). Positive psychology progress: Empirical validation of interventions. *American Psychologist*, 60(5), 410–421.

Severson, J. (2020) *Thrive.* Speaker Sisters.

Sheldon, K., & Lyubomirsky, S. (2019). Revisiting the sustainable happiness model and pie chart: Can happiness be successfully pursued? *The Journal of Positive Psychology.* DOI: 10.1080/17439760.2019.1689421

Sinek, S. (2009). *Start with Why.* New York: Portfolio Press.

Souers, K., & Hall, P. (2016). *Fostering Resilient Learners: Strategies for Creating a Trauma-Sensitive Classroom.* Alexandria, VA: ASCD.

Steptoe, A., O'Donnell, K., Badrick, E., Kumari, M., & Marmot, M. (2008). Neuroendocrine and inflammatory factors associated with positive affect in healthy men and women: The Whitehall II study. *American Journal of Epidemiology*, 167(1), 96–102. DOI: 10.1093/aje/kwm252

Stranges, S. (2014). Major health-related behaviours and mental well-being in the general population: The Health Survey for England. *BMJ Open*, 4(9), e005878.

Summerville, A., & Roese, N. J. (2008). Dare to compare: Fact-based versus simulation-based comparison in daily life. *Journal of Experimental Social Psychology*, 44(3), 664–671. DOI: 10.1016/j.jesp.2007.04.002

Thomas, K., & Kilmann, R. (1978). Comparison of four instruments measuring conflict behavior. *Psychological Reports*, 42(3 Suppl), 1139–1145. DOI: 10.2466/pr0.1978.42.3c.1139

Thomsen, K. (2002). *Building Resilient Students: Integrating Resiliency into What You Already Know and Do.* Thousand Oaks, CA: Corwin.

Triarico, D. (2015). *The Zen Teacher.* San Diego, CA: Dave Burgess Consulting.

Tugade, M., & Fredrickson, B. (2004). Resilient individuals use positive emotions to bounce back from negative emotional experiences. *Journal of Personality and Social Psychology*, 86(2), 320–333. DOI: 10.1037/0022-3514.86.2.320

Tyng, C., Amin, H., Saad, M. & Malik, A. (2017). The influences of emotion on learning and memory. *Frontiers in Psychology*. DOI: 10.3389/fpsyg.2017.01454

University of Haifa. (2017). Blue light emitted by screens damages our sleep, study suggests. *ScienceDaily*. Retrieved April 11, 2020 from www.sciencedaily.com/releases/2017/08/170822103434.htm

van Pragg, H., Fleshner, M., Schwartz, M., & Mattson, M. (2014). Exercise, energy intake, glucose homeostasis, and the brain. *Journal of Neuroscience*, 34(46), 15139–15149. DOI: 10.1523/JNEUROSCI.2814-14.2014

Wiggins, G. (2012). Seven keys to effective feedback. *Educational Leadership*, 70(1), 10–16.

Wilson, T. (2011). *Redirect – The Surprising New Science of Psychological Change*. New York: Little Brown.

Worley, S. (2018). The extraordinary importance of sleep: The detrimental effects of inadequate sleep on health and public safety drive an explosion of sleep research. *P & T: A Peer-Reviewed Journal for Formulary Management*, 43(12), 758–763.

Zahn, R., Moll, J., Paiva, M., Garrido, G., Krueger, F., Huey, E. D., & Grafman, J. (2009). The neural basis of human social values: Evidence from functional MRI. *Cerebral Cortex* (New York, NY: 1991), 19(2), 276–283. DOI: 10.1093/cercor/bhn080

Ziglar, Z. (1977). *See You at the Top*. Gretna, LA: Pelican Press.

For Product Safety Concerns and Information please contact our EU
representative GPSR@taylorandfrancis.com
Taylor & Francis Verlag GmbH, Kaufingerstraße 24, 80331 München, Germany

www.ingramcontent.com/pod-product-compliance
Ingram Content Group UK Ltd.
Pitfield, Milton Keynes, MK11 3LW, UK
UKHW021435080625
459435UK00011B/268